CompTIA ITF+ Exam

450 Questions for Guaranteed Success

Exam Code: FC0-U61

1st Edition

www.versatileread.com

Document Control

Proposal Name	:	CompTIA ITF+ Exam: 450 Questions Guaranteed Success
Document Edition	:	1st
Document Release Date	:	7th August 2024
Reference	:	ITF+ (Exam FC0-U61)
VR Product Code	:	20242802ITF+

Feedback:

If you have any comments regarding the quality of this book or otherwise alter it to better suit your needs, you can contact us through email at info@versatileread.com

Please make sure to include the book's title and ISBN in your message.

VERSAtile Reads

Voice of the Customer: Thank you for choosing this VersatileRead.com product! We highly value your feedback and insights via email to info@versatileread.com. As a token of appreciation, an amazing discount for your next purchase will be sent in response to your email.

About the Contributors:

Nouman Ahmed Khan

AWS/Azure/GCP-Architect, CCDE, CCIEx5 (R&S, SP, Security, DC, Wireless), CISSP, CISA, CISM, CRISC, ISO27K-LA is a Solution Architect working with a global telecommunication provider. He works with enterprises, mega-projects, and service providers to help them select the best-fit technology solutions. He also works as a consultant to understand customer business processes and helps select an appropriate technology strategy to support business goals. He has more than eighteen years of experience working with global clients. One of his notable experiences was his tenure with a large managed security services provider, where he was responsible for managing the complete MSSP product portfolio. With his extensive knowledge and expertise in various areas of technology, including cloud computing, network infrastructure, security, and risk management, Nouman has become a trusted advisor for his clients.

Abubakar Saeed

Abubakar Saeed is a trailblazer in the realm of technology and innovation. With a rich professional journey spanning over twenty-nine years, Abubakar has seamlessly blended his expertise in engineering with his passion for transformative leadership. Starting humbly at the grassroots level, he has significantly contributed to pioneering the Internet in Pakistan and beyond. Abubakar's multifaceted experience encompasses managing, consulting, designing, and implementing projects, showcasing his versatility as a leader.

His exceptional skills shine in leading businesses, where he champions innovation and transformation. Abubakar stands as a testament to the power of visionary leadership, heading operations, solutions design, and integration. His emphasis on adhering to project timelines and exceeding customer expectations has set him apart as a great leader. With an unwavering commitment to adopting technology for operational simplicity and enhanced efficiency, Abubakar Saeed continues to inspire and drive change in the industry.

Dr. Fahad Abdali

Dr. Fahad Abdali is an esteemed leader with an outstanding twenty-year track record in managing diverse businesses. With a stellar educational background, including a bachelor's degree from the prestigious NED University of Engineers & Technology and a Ph.D. from the University of Karachi, Dr. Abdali epitomizes academic excellence and continuous professional growth.

Dr. Abdali's leadership journey is marked by his unwavering commitment to innovation and his astute understanding of industry dynamics. His ability to navigate intricate challenges has driven growth and nurtured organizational triumph. Driven by a passion for excellence, he stands as a beacon of inspiration within the business realm. With his remarkable leadership skills, Dr. Fahad Abdali continues to steer businesses toward unprecedented success, making him a true embodiment of a great leader.

Saba Badar

As an aspiring content developer, Saba is passionate about crafting engaging and informative content that resonates with diverse audiences. With a keen eye for detail and a creative flair, she aims to produce high-quality content that drives results. Saba is dedicated to delivering content that educates, entertains, and inspires.

Table of Contents

About CompTIA IT Fundamentals (ITF+) Exam 7

Introduction 7

What is CompTIA? 7

The Leader in IT Certifications 8

CompTIA Certifications 9

Understanding the Importance of CompTIA ITF+ Certification 11

Why Should You Get This Certification? 13

Prerequisites... 14

What Skills Will You Learn? 14

Who is this Course for? 15

How Does CompTIA ITF+ Certification Help?....................... 15

How Challenging is the CompTIA ITF+ Certification?.......... 15

How Should One Prepare for the CompTIA ITF+ Exam?...... 16

Exam Information... 17

CompTIA ITF+ Purchase Options 17

Certification Renewal 19

Career Growth CompTIA ITF+ Certification in 2024.............................. 19

Practice Questions... 20

Answers 101

About Our Products 184

About CompTIA IT Fundamentals (ITF+) Exam

Introduction

In the vast and dynamic realm of Information Technology, navigating the path to success requires not only technical prowess but also the validation of one's skills by industry-recognized certifications. At the forefront of this validation is CompTIA, an organization synonymous with excellence in IT certifications.

This chapter serves as a gateway into the world of CompTIA, exploring its origins, mission, and the extensive range of certifications it offers. From the foundational CompTIA IT Fundamentals (ITF+) certification to the pinnacle of expertise, we will uncover these credentials' significance in shaping IT professionals' careers worldwide. As we embark on this journey, we will unravel the reasons behind CompTIA's prominence, understand the prerequisites for certification, and explore the tangible benefits of obtaining the CompTIA ITF+ certification.

What is CompTIA?

CompTIA, the Computing Technology Industry Association, stands as a stalwart in the ever-expanding landscape of Information Technology. Established in 1982, this non-profit trade association has become a cornerstone in shaping the IT industry by providing a platform for collaboration, education, and standardization.

At its core, CompTIA acts as a unifying force, bringing together IT professionals, businesses, and educators under a shared umbrella of knowledge and innovation. The organization's mission is multi-faceted, encompassing the advancement of the IT industry, fostering best practices, and providing globally recognized certifications that validate the skills and expertise of professionals at various stages of their careers.

CompTIA's influence extends across the globe, with a reach that spans industries, government entities, and educational institutions. Its commitment to inclusivity and accessibility is reflected in the diverse array of certifications it offers, catering to individuals with varying levels of experience and expertise, covering areas such as cybersecurity, network infrastructure, cloud computing, and more.

CompTIA provides certification examinations, hosts forums and summits globally, leads international policy endeavors, and extends membership to IT companies across diverse disciplines. Renowned for its training initiatives and certification exams, CompTIA has established itself as an industry benchmark. Membership in CompTIA offers the IT community valuable benefits, including access to industry research, networking events, business tools, and educational resources. Additionally, members enjoy discounts on certifications and study materials.

The Leader in IT Certifications

In the fast-paced landscape of Information Technology, one name stands out as the unequivocal leader in the realm of certifications—CompTIA. As a pioneering force, CompTIA has redefined industry standards and set the benchmark for excellence in IT certifications.

- **Setting the Standard:** CompTIA certifications have become synonymous with proficiency and expertise, setting the standard for IT professionals globally. The organization's rigorous certification processes and cutting-edge content ensure that those who hold CompTIA certifications are not only knowledgeable but also equipped with the skills demanded by the ever-evolving tech landscape.
- **Comprehensive Certification Portfolio:** From foundational certifications for beginners to advanced credentials for seasoned professionals, CompTIA offers a comprehensive suite of certifications that caters to diverse skill levels and IT domains. This breadth ensures that individuals can embark on a continuous learning journey, enhancing their expertise at every career stage.
- **Industry-Driven Innovation:** CompTIA does not just keep pace with industry trends; it drives innovation. The organization actively collaborates with industry experts, continually updating its certifications to reflect the latest technologies and best practices. This forward-

thinking approach ensures that CompTIA-certified professionals are at the forefront of technological advancements.

- **Global Recognition:** CompTIA certifications are not confined by geographical borders. They are recognized and respected worldwide, making them a valuable asset for professionals seeking international opportunities. The global recognition of CompTIA certifications opens doors to a myriad of career possibilities and ensures that certified individuals are competitive on a global scale.
- **Career Catalyst:** Beyond being a certification body, CompTIA functions as a career catalyst. The certifications offered by CompTIA are not just badges; they are career milestones. Holding a CompTIA certification signifies technical proficiency, a commitment to excellence, and a dedication to adapting seamlessly in a rapidly changing industry.

CompTIA Certifications

- **ITF+:** IT Fundamentals (ITF+) encompasses a distinctive range of IT subjects, offering a comprehensive foundation in the technological concepts and practices prevalent in contemporary organizational settings.
- **A+:** A+ is the initial stepping stone for those entering the IT field, with performance-based exams certifying fundamental IT skills applicable across various devices and operating systems.
- **Network+:** Network+ attests to the crucial skills needed to confidently design, configure, manage, and troubleshoot both wired and wireless devices.
- **Security+:** The Security+ certification is an internationally recognized credential that confirms the fundamental abilities needed to carry out essential security tasks and advance in the IT security profession.
- **Cloud+:** Cloud+ validates the expertise necessary to securely implement, maintain, and leverage cloud technologies.
- **Linux+:** Linux+ is an internationally recognized certification affirming the technical competencies essential for junior-level Linux administrators.

- **Server+:** Server+ showcases the technical knowledge and skills required to perform diverse server platform tasks.
- **CySA+:** Cybersecurity Analyst (CySA+) applies behavioral analytics to enhance the overall state of IT security within the cybersecurity field.
- **CASP+:** CASP+ represents an advanced certification validating critical thinking and judgment across various security disciplines in complex environments.
- **PenTest+:** CompTIA PenTest+ targets intermediate-level cybersecurity professionals engaged in penetration testing to address network vulnerabilities.
- **Data+:** CompTIA Data+ is an early-career data analytics certification that instills confidence in applying data analysis to real-world scenarios and facilitating data-driven business decisions.
- **DataSys+:** CompTIA DataSys+ covers the knowledge and skills needed to deploy, maintain, and safeguard data businesses and organizations collect.
- **Project+:** Project+ verifies the ability to initiate, manage, and successfully complete projects or business initiatives within specified timelines and budgets.
- **CTT+:** CTT+ certifies knowledge and proficiency in tools and techniques essential for effective teaching in contemporary learning environments.
- **Cloud Essentials+:** Cloud Essentials+ demonstrates that IT and non-technical professionals possess the business acumen required to make informed decisions and recommendations regarding cloud services.

VERSAtile Reads

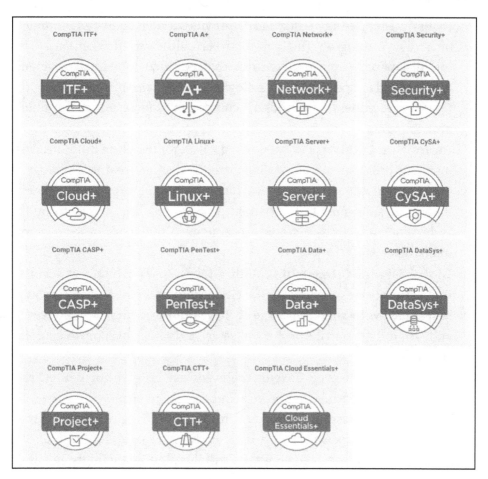

Understanding the Importance of CompTIA ITF+ Certification

Beyond the conventional reasons, CompTIA IT Fundamentals (ITF+) certification holds distinct importance in IT education and professional development. Let's explore some unique aspects that set ITF+ apart:

- **Digital Literacy Empowerment:** ITF+ goes beyond technical skills; it empowers individuals with digital literacy. Covering fundamental IT concepts equips professionals and enthusiasts with the ability to navigate the digital landscape, fostering a society where everyone can participate meaningfully in the digital era.

- **Holistic Technology Grasp:** ITF+ provides a holistic understanding of technology, bridging the gap between different IT domains. This interdisciplinary approach ensures that certified individuals not only comprehend specific technologies but also recognize the interconnectedness of various IT components, fostering well-rounded professionals.

- **Innovation Catalyst:** ITF+ acts as a catalyst for fostering innovation. By instilling problem-solving skills and encouraging creative thinking, it prepares individuals to adapt to evolving technologies and contribute to innovative solutions. ITF+ certified professionals are poised to be the architects of technological advancements, driving innovation across industries.

- **Global Digital Citizenship:** With a focus on IT ethics and security, ITF+ promotes responsible digital citizenship on a global scale. It equips individuals with the knowledge to navigate the digital world securely and ethically, contributing to a safer and more responsible online community.

- **Empowering Diverse Career Trajectories:** ITF+ is not limited to a specific career path. It empowers individuals to explore diverse roles within the IT landscape. Whether someone is aspiring to be a developer, a cybersecurity specialist, or a data analyst, ITF+ fulfills the role of a versatile foundation, allowing for flexibility and adaptability in career choices.

- **Community Building:** ITF+ fosters a sense of community among learners. As individuals embark on their IT journey, the shared experience of mastering foundational concepts creates a community of practice. This community becomes a valuable resource for ongoing learning, collaboration, and support.

- **Elevating Digital Confidence:** ITF+ boosts digital confidence. Through practical knowledge and hands-on skills, it empowers individuals to troubleshoot common IT issues independently, fostering a culture of self-reliance and digital empowerment.

- **Gateway to Lifelong Learning:** ITF+ is not a one-time achievement but a gateway to lifelong learning. It establishes a continuous improvement mindset, encouraging individuals to stay curious, explore new technologies, and pursue advanced certifications, ensuring relevance in an ever-changing IT landscape.

Why Should You Get This Certification?

Did you know that the field of IT is anticipated to expand at an almost double rate compared to the national growth estimate? Tech occupations are predicted to be among the most rapidly growing sectors from 2024 to 2033, according to the U.S. Bureau of Labor Statistics.

A significant majority of employers globally, approximately 72%, consider technology a key factor in achieving business objectives, as per CompTIA's International Trends in Technology and Workforce. This underscores the essential need for all individuals to possess fundamental IT skills to effectively utilize these technologies in the workplace.

Obtaining CompTIA IT Fundamentals (ITF+) certification offers numerous benefits, including the acquisition of fundamental technological proficiencies and enduring capabilities, making it a valuable investment in your IT journey. Here are compelling reasons why you should consider pursuing ITF+ certification:

1. **Foundational Knowledge:** ITF+ provides a solid understanding of fundamental IT concepts, including hardware, software, networking, and security, serving as a cornerstone for further learning.

2. **Career Entry:** Ideal for beginners, ITF+ acts as a gateway into the IT industry, opening doors to entry-level positions and paving the way for career progression.

3. **Global Recognition:** CompTIA certifications, like ITF+, are globally recognized, enhancing your marketability and making you a competitive candidate worldwide.

4. **Versatility:** Covering a broad range of IT topics, ITF+ equips you with versatile skills, allowing exploration of various IT domains and specialization paths.

5. Professional Development: ITF+ is committed to ongoing professional development, showcasing proactive learning and adaptability in a dynamic IT landscape.

Prerequisites

CompTIA certifications, including CompTIA IT Fundamentals (ITF+), do not have strict age requirements or educational prerequisites. However, CompTIA does recommend that candidates be at least 13 years old before attempting to take any CompTIA exam. This recommendation ensures that individuals have a foundational level of maturity and understanding to effectively engage with the certification material.

This inclusivity in age requirements aligns with CompTIA's commitment to making IT certifications accessible to a diverse audience, including students, professionals, and individuals at various stages of their careers. It emphasizes that the focus is on skills and knowledge rather than specific age or educational backgrounds.

What Skills Will You Learn?

- **IT Concepts and Language:** Understanding symbolic systems, fundamental computing principles, the significance of data, and techniques for problem-solving.
- **Infrastructure:** Arranging and configuring typical peripheral devices for a laptop/PC or establishing the security of a basic wireless network.
- **Applications and Programs:** Software applications, the essential elements of an operating system, and the objectives behind various approaches to application architecture.
- **Software Development:** Categories of programming languages, logical structures, and the intentions behind programming concepts.
- **Foundations of Databases:** Principles, structures, and purposes of databases, along with the approaches used to interact with them.
- **Security:** Addressing concerns related to confidentiality, integrity, and availability in secure devices, along with best practices for ensuring security.

Who is this Course for?

This course is tailored for:

- Students and individuals contemplating a career switch with aspirations in the IT field
- Professionals operating in sectors demanding a comprehensive understanding of IT
- Marketing, sales, and operations staff seeking to elevate job performance, boost technological proficiency, and decrease dependency on IT support

How Does CompTIA ITF+ Certification Help?

CompTIA IT Fundamentals (ITF+) Certification stands out as a dynamic enabler, providing a transformative journey into the intricate landscape of Information Technology. Beyond traditional certifications, ITF+ serves as a comprehensive guide, offering a profound understanding of IT fundamentals while fostering innovative problem-solving skills. It acts as a compass for career seekers and changers, uniquely aligning them with the intricacies of the IT industry. For professionals in various domains, ITF+ serves as a bridge, transcending conventional IT boundaries and amplifying their capabilities. Marketing, sales, and operations staff discover a unique pathway to elevate job performance, enhancing technological prowess and a holistic approach to efficiency. In essence, CompTIA ITF+ Certification is not merely a validation of skills; it is a distinctive initiation into a realm of limitless possibilities and multidimensional professional development.

How Challenging is the CompTIA ITF+ Certification?

The challenge posed by the CompTIA IT Fundamentals (ITF+) Certification is akin to a strategic journey rather than an unbeatable obstacle. Designed as an entry-level certification, ITF+ strikes a balance between depth and accessibility. It challenges individuals to master foundational IT concepts, providing a comprehensive understanding without overwhelming complexity. The exam assesses proficiency in areas such as IT basics, infrastructure, applications, software development, databases, and security.

While demanding, the certification's structured curriculum ensures that candidates with dedication and a methodical approach can confidently navigate and conquer its challenges. ITF+ provides an invigorating introduction to the world of IT certifications, making the journey both challenging and immensely rewarding for those embarking on it.

How Should One Prepare for the CompTIA ITF+ Exam?

Preparing for the CompTIA IT Fundamentals (ITF+) exam involves a strategic and methodical approach to ensure success.

- Begin by familiarizing yourself with the exam objectives, which outline the key topics to be covered.
- Utilize CompTIA's official study materials, including books, online courses, and practice exams, to deepen your understanding of IT concepts, infrastructure, applications, software development, databases, and security.
- Engage in hands-on activities, such as setting up a basic network or troubleshooting common IT issues, to reinforce theoretical knowledge.
- Additionally, explore supplementary resources, join online forums, and consider participating in study groups to benefit from diverse perspectives and shared insights.
- Regularly assess your progress through practice exams to identify areas that require further attention. By adopting a well-rounded study plan, incorporating practical experience, and leveraging available resources, you can confidently approach the ITF+ exam and enhance your readiness for success.

Exam Information

Prior Certification		Exam Validity	
Not Required		3 Years	
Exam Fee		Exam Duration	
$130 USD		60 Minutes	
No. of Questions		Passing Marks	
75 Questions		650 (on a scale of 900)	

Recommended Experience

The CompTIA IT Fundamentals (ITF+) exam focuses on the knowledge and skills required to identify and explain the basics of Computing, IT Infrastructure, Software Development and Database use.

Exam Format

Multiple Choice

CompTIA ITF+ Purchase Options

The CompTIA ITF+ certification is priced at $200, covering the cost of the exam voucher necessary to take the examination. Vouchers can be acquired directly from CompTIA or through authorized resellers.

The exam cost may vary based on the voucher purchase location, and additional fees for testing center accommodations or supplementary services may apply.

There are five main CompTIA ITF+ purchase options:

Exam Voucher Only:

o   This is the most basic option and includes only the exam voucher.
o   The cost of a voucher is **$134.**

Basic Bundle:

o   This bundle includes the exam voucher and a self-paced study guide.

o   The cost of the Basic Bundle is **$205.**

Exam Prep Bundle:

o   This bundle includes the exam voucher, a self-paced study guide, and CompTIA CertMaster Practice.
o   The cost of the Exam Prep Bundle is **$256.**

eLearning Bundle:

o   This bundle includes the exam voucher, a self-paced study guide, CompTIA CertMaster Practice, and integrated CertMaster Learn and CompTIA Labs.
o   The cost of the eLearning Bundle is **$411.**

Complete Bundle:

o   This bundle includes the exam voucher, a self-paced study guide, CompTIA CertMaster Practice, integrated CertMaster Learn and CompTIA Labs, and CompTIA CertMaster Practice.
o   The cost of the Complete Bundle is **$473.**

In addition to these four main options, there are also a number of other CompTIA ITF+ training materials available, including instructor-led training, virtual labs, and practice questions. You can find more information about these options on the CompTIA website (https://www.comptia.org/certifications/it-fundamentals)

Option	Price (USD)	Description	Includes
Exam Voucher Only	$134.00	Starting at $13/mo with affirm (USA only)	• Exam Voucher
Basic Bundle	$205.00	Starting at $19/mo with affirm (USA only)	• Exam Voucher + Retake • Self-Paced Study Guide
Exam Prep Bundle	$256.00	Starting at $24/mo with affirm (USA only)	• Exam Voucher + Retake • Self-Paced Study Guide • CompTIA CertMaster Practice

eLearning Bundle	$411.00	Starting at $38/mo with affirm (USA only)	• Exam Voucher + Retake • Integrated CertMaster Learn + CompTIA Labs
Complete Bundle	$473.00	Starting at $43/mo with affirm (USA only)	• Exam Voucher + Retake • Integrated CertMaster Learn + CompTIA Labs • CompTIA CertMaster Practice

Certification Renewal

The CompTIA ITF+ certification is considered good for life and does not need to be renewed. This means that once you pass the exam, you are certified for life.

However, CompTIA does recommend that you stay up-to-date on the latest IT trends and technologies by completing continuing education (CE) activities. This will not only help you sustain and enhance your skills and knowledge but also elevate your competitiveness in the job market.

There are a number of ways to earn CEUs for the CompTIA ITF+ certification, including:

• Attending industry events and conferences
• Taking online and in-person training courses
• Reading IT books and articles
• Participating in webinars and online forums

You can submit your CEU documentation to CompTIA to track your progress. Although Continuing Education Units (CEUs) are not mandatory for the renewal of your ITF+ certification, they can be advantageous in preserving your expertise, enhancing your knowledge, and propelling your career forward.

Career Growth CompTIA ITF+ Certification in 2024

The CompTIA ITF+ certification is a foundational IT certification that can help you launch a career in the IT industry. In 2024, the IT industry is expected to grow by 11%, creating more than 900,000 new jobs. This makes it a great time to get certified in CompTIA ITF+.

Practice Questions

1. Which type of computer is housed in a case that can sit on or under a desk?
A) Laptop
B) Desktop
C) Server
D) Tablet

2. What term is often used interchangeably with 'desktop computer'?
A) Laptop
B) Workstation
C) Server
D) Tablet

3. What is a particularly powerful type of desktop computer commonly referred to as?
A) Laptop
B) Workstation
C) Server
D) Tablet

4. What is contained within the computer's case and connected to the motherboard via ports?
A) Network cable
B) Peripheral devices
C) Wireless adapter
D) External hard drive

5. Which peripheral device is essential for input?
A) Printer
B) Mouse
C) Speaker
D) Webcam

6. What does a higher specification CPU improve in a workstation-class computer?
A) Power consumption
B) Data processing speed
C) Portability
D) Battery life

7. What determines the basic speed of a computer?
A) RAM size
B) CPU speed
C) Hard drive capacity
D) Monitor size

8. What type of storage drive is replacing legacy hard drives due to performance?
A) Solid State Drive (SSD)
B) Floppy disk
C) CD-ROM
D) USB flash drive

9. What is the main difference between the components of a server and a desktop?
A) Servers use wireless components
B) Server components are more powerful and reliable
C) Desktops can support more users simultaneously
D) Servers are portable

10. What is a critical design feature for servers to ensure reliability?
A) Lower power consumption
B) High-quality components and redundancy
C) Touchscreen interface
D) Lightweight design

11. What is the term for a portable computer integrating display, system

components, and input/output devices within a single case?
A) Desktop
B) Server
C) Laptop
D) Workstation

12. What is the typical weight range for laptops?
A) 1 to 4 kg
B) 5 to 9 kg
C) 10 to 14 kg
D) 15 to 20 kg

13. What type of display technology do laptops use?
A) CRT
B) Flat-panel display
C) Plasma screen
D) OLED

14. What is the primary power source for portable computers?
A) Solar power
B) Internal battery packs
C) External power supply
D) Wind energy

15. What type of networking technology do portable computers primarily use?
A) Ethernet cables
B) Wireless radio technologies
C) Fiber optic cables
D) Dial-up modems

16. Which term is used for smaller laptops?
A) Desktop replacements
B) Notebooks
C) Mainframes

D) Supercomputers

17. What operating system do Apple Macintosh computers use?
A) Windows
B) Linux
C) Chrome OS
D) macOS

18. What is the distinguishing feature of an all-in-one PC?
A) Components are contained within the monitor case
B) It uses a server motherboard
C) It has no display screen
D) It is battery-powered

19. What makes a server system fault-tolerant?
A) Single high-quality component
B) Extra copies of components
C) Lightweight design
D) Built-in touchscreen

20. What kind of case do server computers often use?
A) Portable case
B) Rack-mountable case
C) All-in-one case
D) Standard desktop case

21. What is an example of a software server?
A) Printer server
B) Web server
C) Mouse server
D) Display server

22. What type of laptops can be used, such as a tablet?
A) Desktop replacements
B) Hybrid laptops

C) Subnotebooks

D) Mainframes

23. Which company is not a dominant player in the global PC market?

A) Dell

B) HP/Compaq

C) Lenovo

D) Microsoft

24. What does the quality of peripherals affect in a computer?

A) Power consumption

B) Ergonomics

C) Storage capacity

D) Network speed

25. What type of laptop meets Intel's specifications for performance, size/weight, and battery life?

A) Notebook

B) Ultrabook

C) Hybrid laptop

D) Desktop replacement

26. Which component has a significant impact on system speed besides the CPU?

A) Monitor size

B) Main storage drive type and speed

C) Keyboard type

D) Mouse sensitivity

27. Which device can be considered optional for a desktop PC?

A) Monitor

B) Keyboard

C) Printer

D) Mouse

28. What is the purpose of a sound card in a desktop PC?
A) To improve data processing speed
B) To allow audio playback
C) To connect to the internet
D) To increase storage capacity

29. What impacts the performance of a desktop PC the most?
A) Monitor size
B) CPU speed and system memory
C) Keyboard layout
D) Mouse sensitivity

30. What type of computers are servers compared to desktops?
A) Less reliable
B) More expensive and reliable
C) Portable
D) Battery-powered

31. What is the main feature of rack-mountable server cases?
A) Portable
B) Easy to expand and upgrade
C) Integrated display
D) Touchscreen interface

32. What does a higher capacity main storage drive allow a computer to do?
A) Process data faster
B) Store more data when switched off
C) Connect to multiple networks
D) Improve battery life

33. Which company is known for shipping Macintosh computers?
A) Dell
B) HP
C) Lenovo

D) Apple

34. What is a major advantage of desktop PCs?
A) Fixed design
B) Modifiable design with various components
C) Lightweight
D) Portability

35. Which type of computer is typically used as a network client to access shared resources?
A) Server
B) Desktop PC
C) Tablet
D) Mainframe

36. What is the main distinguishing feature of a hybrid laptop?
A) Fixed display
B) Can be used as a tablet
C) Rack-mountable case
D) Uses CRT display

37. Which tab in File Explorer options allows you to reset view settings on a per-folder basis?
A) General
B) View
C) Security
D) Advanced

38. What is an important factor in a computer's graphics subsystem?
A) Monitor size
B) Graphics subsystem type and speed
C) Keyboard layout
D) Mouse sensitivity

39. What is the main use of a printer connected to a desktop PC?

A) Input
B) Output
C) Processing
D) Storage

40. What type of computer often uses a special case designed to fit into a steel rack shelving system?
A) Desktop PC
B) Server
C) Laptop
D) Tablet

41. Which term refers to laptops meeting specific performance and size/weight criteria?
A) Desktop replacement
B) Notebook
C) Ultrabook
D) Mainframe

42. What is the function of system memory in a computer?
A) Store data when switched off
B) Run applications and process data more quickly
C) Display images
D) Connect to the internet

43. What is the advantage of using wireless radio technologies in portable computers?
A) Faster data processing
B) Mobility and ease of connectivity
C) Lower cost
D) Increased storage capacity

44. Which component is integrated into laptops but not typically desktops?
A) Keyboard
B) Touchpad

C) Monitor

D) CPU

45. Which of the following best describes the role of an interpreter in programming?

A) Translates high-level code into machine code in one go

B) Converts high-level code into an intermediate bytecode

C) Translates and executes high-level code line by line

D) Compiles high-level code into assembly language

46. Which type of computer is known for supporting many users simultaneously?

A) Desktop PC

B) Server

C) Laptop

D) Tablet

47. What type of laptop is often called a desktop replacement?

A) Hybrid laptop

B) Larger, more powerful laptops

C) Notebook

D) Subnotebook

48. Which component in a server system is often duplicated for fault tolerance?

A) Monitor

B) CPU

C) Hard drive

D) Keyboard

49. What is the main purpose of a web server?

A) Display images

B) Serve web pages to users

C) Print documents

D) Store files

50. What does the term OEM stand for?
A) Original Equipment Manufacturer
B) Online Equipment Manager
C) Office Equipment Mechanic
D) Overhead Equipment Maintenance

51. Which type of device is typically used for data input in a desktop PC?
A) Monitor
B) Keyboard
C) Speaker
D) Printer

52. What is the primary feature of a Chromebook?
A) Runs Chrome OS
B) Uses Mac OS
C) Battery-powered
D) Touchscreen interface

53. What is the weight range for a typical desktop replacement laptop?
A) 1 to 2 kg
B) 3 to 4 kg
C) 5 to 9 kg
D) 10 to 15 kg

54. Which company is a strong player in the laptop and hybrid markets?
A) Acer
B) IBM
C) Cisco
D) Oracle

55. Which term describes a smaller, lighter laptop often used for portability?
A) Mainframe
B) Notebook

C) Supercomputer

D) Workstation

56. What is the role of a database server?

A) Display images

B) Serve database queries to users

C) Print documents

D) Store files

57. Which type of computer is most likely to have a built-in battery?

A) Desktop PC

B) Server

C) Laptop

D) Mainframe

58. Which of the following types of cables is typically used for high-speed data transmission over short distances and is known for its immunity to electromagnetic interference?

A) Coaxial cable

B) Twisted pair cable

C) Fiber optic cable

D) USB cable

59. Which company is not listed as a dominant player in the server market?

A) Dell

B) HPE (HP Enterprise)

C) Lenovo

D) Apple

60. Which of the following best describes the purpose of a device driver?

A) A program that controls the basic functions of an operating system

B) Software that manages the hardware components of a computer

C) A utility that diagnoses and repairs hardware issues

D) An application that provides an interface for users to perform specific tasks

VERSAtile Reads

61. What is the primary role of an Operating System (OS)?
A) To provide hardware components
B) To serve as an interface between the user, hardware, and applications
C) To manufacture computer hardware
D) To create application software

62. What type of interface did the earliest operating systems for PCs, such as DOS, use?
A) Graphical User Interface (GUI)
B) Command-line interface
C) Touchscreen interface
D) Voice-controlled interface

63. Windows is sometimes described as a:
A) WIMP interface
B) MOUSE interface
C) TOUCH interface
D) VOICE interface

64. What does the OS software "kernel" provide?
A) User manuals
B) Core functions of the OS
C) Application software
D) Peripheral devices

65. What must each hardware component have to function correctly with an OS?
A) A command-line interface
B) A graphical shell
C) A driver
D) A kernel

66. Most CPUs released in the last few years can work in which modes?
A) 16-bit and 32-bit

B) 32-bit and 64-bit
C) 64-bit and 128-bit
D) 8-bit and 16-bit

67. What can a computer with a 64-bit CPU run?
A) Only 64-bit operating systems
B) Only 32-bit operating systems
C) Both 64-bit and 32-bit operating systems
D) Only 16-bit operating systems

68. What is application software?
A) Programs that allow users to perform different tasks
B) The kernel of the OS
C) Peripheral devices
D) Hardware components

69. Changes to an operating system must be made carefully to:
A) Improve graphics
B) Enhance hardware compatibility
C) Remain compatible with previous generations of software and hardware
D) Increase its cost

70. What does an OS use to organize files on a storage device?
 A) Command-line interface
 B) Directory (or folder) structure
 C) Peripheral devices
 D) Kernel functions

71. Which of the following is an example of a workstation OS?
 A) Apple iOS
 B) Microsoft Windows
 C) UNIX
 D) Android

72. What type of OS is designed for handheld devices?

A) Server OS
B) Workstation OS
C) Mobile Device OS
D) Embedded OS

73. What does Apple develop the principal mobile operating system?
A) Android
B) iOS
C) Windows Mobile
D) Symbian

74. A server OS is likely to include:
A) A full GUI
B) Peripheral devices
C) Software packages to run network services
D) Only 32-bit support

75. What is an open-source operating system?
A) A system where the programming code is kept secret
B) A system where the programming code is freely available
C) A system with no user interface
D) A system that requires a license fee

76. Which of the following is an example of an open-source OS?
A) Microsoft Windows
B) Apple macOS
C) UNIX
D) Apple iOS

77. In an embedded system, what does the OS act as?
A) Application software
B) Peripheral device
C) Firmware
D) Kernel

78. What is the term used for a highly stable and reliable embedded OS platform?
A) Workstation OS
B) Server OS
C) Real -Time Operating System (RTOS)
D) Mobile Device OS

79. What does BIOS stand for?
A) Basic Input/Output System
B) Basic Information Operation System
C) Binary Input/Output System
D) Basic Interface Operating System

80. What kind of firmware might newer motherboards use?
A) DOS
B) BIOS
C) UEFI
D) UNIX

81. Which type of OS cannot typically be uninstalled and replaced with a different OS?
A) Workstation OS
B) Server OS
C) Embedded OS
D) Mobile Device OS

82. What is one consequence of having a common OS environment for application software?
A) Increased hardware costs
B) Simplified application development
C) More frequent hardware failures
D) Decreased software reliability

83. What tool might an OS provide to monitor system health and performance?

A) BIOS
B) Performance monitoring tools
C) Graphical shell
D) Command-line interface

84. Which type of OS is designed to run on servers in business networks?
A) Mobile Device OS
B) Workstation OS
C) Server OS
D) Embedded OS

85. What kind of system is an embedded OS typically used in?
A) General-purpose computer systems
B) Gaming consoles
C) Highly specific function devices
D) Desktop PCs

86. What is a fundamental difference between computer systems?
A) The size of the hard disk
B) The amount of memory
C) The "size" of the instructions the CPU can process
D) The number of peripherals

87. Which of the following security practices involves regularly reviewing and updating user access rights and permissions to ensure the least privilege?

A) Patch management
B) Access control management
C) Incident response planning
D) Network segmentation

88. How does open-source software claim to make improvements available?
A) More slowly and expensively
B) Quickly and cost-effectively

C) Without user feedback

D) Only through updates

89. What is the primary purpose of drivers in an OS?

A) To create application software

B) To identify hardware components

C) To enable the hardware components to function

D) To provide a graphical user interface

90. What does UEFI provide support for that BIOS does not?

A) 32-bit CPU operation at boot

B) A command-line interface at boot

C) 64-bit CPU operation at boot

D) Peripheral device configuration

91. What kind of tasks must many embedded systems perform?

A) Non-time-sensitive tasks

B) Time-sensitive tasks

C) User interface tasks

D) Application software tasks

92. Which OS is described as using a WIMP interface?

A) UNIX

B) Linux

C) Windows

D) Android

93. What is not a characteristic of a Real-Time Operating System (RTOS)?

A) Predictable response times

B) Stability

C) Frequent reboots

D) Reliability

94. What is a kernel in the context of an OS?

A) A type of hardware

B) Core functions of the OS

C) A peripheral device

D) An application software

95. Which operating system is an example of a commercial OS?

A) Linux

B) Android

C) UNIX

D) Apple macOS

96. What does the OS allow application software developers to do?

A) Write routines to access hardware directly

B) Focus on application functions

C) Manufacture hardware components

D) Design user interfaces

97. What is a common feature of workstation OS?

A) Designed for handheld devices

B) Often used in industrial control systems

C) Can be uninstalled and replaced

D) Designed to run network services

98. What is one role of utility software included with an OS?

A) Manufacture hardware components

B) Configure and monitor the computer

C) Write application software

D) Design user interfaces

99. What does firmware in a PC provide?

A) Application software

B) User interface

C) Low-level interface for the OS to control components

D) Peripheral device management

100. What is the primary role of directory structure in an OS?

A) To organize files on a storage device

B) To create application software

C) To manage peripheral devices

D) To provide core functions of the OS

101. Which versions of Windows can run most 32-bit applications?

A) 32-bit editions

B) 64-bit editions

C) Both 32-bit and 64-bit editions

D) None of the above

102. What is required for 64-bit editions of Windows to run certain hardware devices?

A) 32-bit drivers authorized by Microsoft

B) 64-bit hardware device drivers authorized by Microsoft

C) Any generic drivers

D) No drivers are needed

103. Can a 32-bit version of Windows run 64-bit applications?

A) Yes

B) No

C) Only if the hardware supports it

D) Only with third-party software

104. Which mobile operating systems has Microsoft developed?

A) Windows CE, Windows Phone 7, Windows Phone 8, and Windows 10 Mobile

B) Windows Phone 7, Windows Phone 8, and Windows 9 Mobile

C) Windows Mobile, Windows Phone 7, and Windows 10 Mobile

D) Windows CE, Windows Phone 7, and Windows Mobile

105. What is significant about Windows 10 Mobile's user interface and code base?
A) It is completely different from other Windows versions
B) It is consistent across all types of devices
C) It uses a command-line interface
D) It is only for smartphones

106. Which company developed the Apple Macintosh?
A) Microsoft
B) IBM
C) Apple
D) Google

107. What was revolutionary about the Apple Macintosh when it was first released?
A) It used a command-line interface
B) It had a graphical user interface
C) It was the first computer to use DOS
D) It was developed by IBM

108. What is the main difference between Mac OS and other operating systems?
A) It is available for any computer
B) It is supplied only with Apple-built computers
C) It is less stable than other operating systems
D) It uses a command-line interface

109. From which operating system kernel was macOS re-developed?
A) DOS
C) Linux
B) UNIX
D) Windows

110. How are macOS updates typically released?
 A) Users must purchase each update

B) Updates are released free-of-charge
C) Updates are only for new hardware
D) Updates are not usually released

111. What is iOS primarily known for?
A) Its complexity
B) Its ease of navigation
C) Its command-line interface
D) Its requirement for external keyboards

112. What type of source is iOS?
A) Open-source
B) Closed-source
C) Semi-open source
D) Public domain

113. How is the interface on an iPhone controlled?
A) Using a command-line
B) Using a mouse
C) Entirely via touch
D) Using a keyboard

114. What is the main function of the Home key on an iPhone?
A) To turn the phone on and off
B) To return the user to the Home Screen
C) To adjust the volume
D) To access the internet

115. What is Linux based on?
A) Windows
B) macOS
C) UNIX
D) DOS

116. To delete a file using Explorer, which key should you press after

selecting it?
A) DEL
B) BACKSPACE
C) SHIFT
D) CTRL

117. What type of environment does Chrome OS provide compared to Windows?
A) More complex
B) Minimal
C) Similar
D) Command-line

118. What is a key characteristic of Chrome OS?
A) It is developed by Microsoft
B) It is used mainly for gaming
C) It is designed to use web applications
D) It requires powerful hardware

119. Which company developed Chrome OS?
A) Microsoft
B) Apple
C) Google
D) IBM

120. What is a common use for Linux as a server OS?
A) Desktop applications
B) Web servers
C) Gaming servers
D) Mobile applications

121. Can Chrome OS run Android apps?
A) Yes
B) No
C) Only on Chromebooks

D) Only on Chromeboxes

122. Which of the following is not a version of Windows for mobile devices?
A) Windows CE
B) Windows Phone 7
C) Windows Phone 8
D) Windows XP Mobile

123. What kind of updates does macOS get?
A) Monthly updates
B) "Dot" version updates
C) Weekly updates
D) No updates

124. What does shaking an iOS device activate?
A) Search
B) Undo
C) Shut down
D) Lock screen

125. What is the primary market for Chrome OS hardware?
A) High-end gaming
B) Budget market
C) Enterprise servers
D) Scientific computing

126. If you change a file's extension, what might happen?
A) The file size increases
B) The file will not open with the correct program
C) The file becomes hidden
D) The file becomes read-only

127. Which keyboard shortcut is used to copy a file?
A) CTRL+X
B) CTRL+C

C) CTRL+V

D) CTRL+Z

128. What is a key feature of Apple's OS X/macOS?

A) It is available for purchase separately

B) It is derived from UNIX

C) It does not support older Mac OS applications

D) It uses a command-line interface

129. What is the main benefit of Mac OS being supplied only with Apple-built computers?

A) It makes Mac OS less stable

B) It reduces hardware compatibility

C) It helps to make Mac OS stable

D) It makes Mac OS open source

130. Which of the following vendors does not produce end-user applications for Linux?

A) IBM

B) Sun/Oracle

C) Novell

D) Microsoft

131. Which type of software does Chrome OS primarily use?

A) Desktop applications

B) Web applications

C) Command-line applications

D) Gaming applications

132. What is a common use for Linux in educational institutions?

A) As a server OS

B) For gaming

C) For desktop applications

D) For mobile applications

133. What kind of updates are released for iOS?
A) Paid updates
B) Free updates
C) No updates
D) Only security updates

134. Which type of OS is Linux considered to be?
A) Proprietary
B) Open-source
C) Closed-source
D) Semi-open source

135. Which operating system is known for having a devoted following despite a smaller user base?
A) Windows
B) macOS
C) Linux
D) Chrome OS

136. What is a unique feature of the Mac OS graphical interface?
A) It uses a command-line interface
B) It is derived from DOS
C) It is supplemented with additional code
D) It is compatible with Windows applications

137. What is the primary input method for iOS devices?
A) Mouse
B) Keyboard
C) Touch
D) Voice

138. What can users do by tapping and holding an icon on iOS?
A) Delete the icon
B) Re-arrange icons
C) Access settings

D) Open the app

139. Which company produces Surface tablets?
A) Apple
B) Google
C) Microsoft
D) IBM

140. What kind of apps can Chrome OS run besides web applications?
A) Windows apps
B) macOS apps
C) Linux apps
D) Android apps

141. Which operating system kernel is macOS developed from?
A) Windows
B) UNIX
C) DOS
D) Linux

142. What is the main characteristic of Chrome OS hardware?
A) High-end and expensive
B) Budget and affordable
C) Developed for gaming
D) Enterprise-focused

143. In what context is Linux most widely deployed?
A) Desktop applications
B) Web servers
C) Gaming servers
D) Mobile applications

144. What kind of environment does Chrome OS provide?
A) Complex and feature-rich
B) Minimal and streamlined

C) Similar to Windows

D) Command line only

145. Which operating system does not support a consistent user interface and code base across all device types?
A) Windows 10 Mobile
B) iOS
C) Android
D) Linux

146. What is the first step in the CompTIA Troubleshooting Model?
A) Research knowledge base/internet
B) Identify the problem
C) Establish a theory of probable cause
D) Test the theory to determine the cause

147. Which of the following is not part of the step to identify the problem?
A) Gather information
B) Duplicate the problem, if possible
C) Implement the solution
D) Question users

148. From a business point of view, what is often more important than solving the original cause of a problem?
A) Identifying symptoms
B) Resolving the consequences of the problem
C) Researching knowledge base/Internet
D) Documenting findings/lessons learned

149. When questioning users to identify the problem, which of the following should be avoided?
A) Being polite
B) Blaming the user for causing the problem
C) Addressing questions to the user's level of expertise
D) Asking the user to describe the symptoms

150. What should be done if the theory of probable cause is not confirmed?
A) Establish a new theory or escalate
B) Implement the solution
C) Document findings
D) Verify full system functionality

151. Which of the following is not a technique used to identify the problem?
A) Gather information
B) Duplicate the problem
C) Establish a plan of action
D) Question users

152. What is the purpose of establishing a theory of probable cause?
A) To implement preventive measures
B) To eliminate possible causes through testing
C) To document findings
D) To escalate the issue

153. What should you do if you discover symptoms of more than one problem?
A) Treat each issue as a separate case
B) Implement the solution immediately
C) Ignore one of the problems
D) Roll back recent changes

154. What is the importance of determining if anything has changed when identifying the problem?
A) To duplicate the problem
B) To identify potential causes of the problem
C) To establish a new theory
D) To escalate the issue

155. After implementing the solution, what is the next step in the troubleshooting process?
A) Document findings

B) Identify the problem

C) Verify full system functionality

D) Research knowledge base

156. Which of the following data types is most appropriate for storing a person's age in years?

A) Float

B) Integer

C) String

D) Boolean

157. What is a common cause of problems that occur after a change?
A) Password expiration
B) Configuration change
C) Duplicate problems
D) Identical symptoms

158. Which step involves determining the next steps to resolve the problem after confirming the root cause?
A) Establish a theory of probable cause
B) Test the theory to determine the cause
C) Establish a plan of action
D) Implement preventive measures

159. What is the first action to take when encountering a troubleshooting situation?
A) Establish a plan of action
B) Identify the problem
C) Implement the solution
D) Document findings

160. What is the purpose of questioning users during the troubleshooting process?

VERSAtile Reads

A) To blame them for the problem
B) To gather information about the problem
C) To document findings
D) To escalate the issue

161. What key should you press to rename a file after selecting it?
A) F1
B) F2
C) F3
D) F4

162. What should be done if the problem cannot be duplicated on a reference system?
A) Treat it as a separate case
B) Focus on the user's local environment
C) Ignore the problem
D) Implement the solution immediately

163. Which key combination allows you to select a block of files using the keyboard?
A) CTRL + ARROW keys
B) SHIFT + ARROW keys
C) ALT + ARROW keys
D) SHIFT + SPACEBAR

164. What is the importance of monitoring other support requests?
A) To escalate the issue
B) To identify similar problems
C) To document findings
D) To implement preventive measures

165. What is the first method to gather information about a problem?
A) Use a remote desktop tool
B) View system log files
C) Question the user

D) Monitor other support requests

166. During which step do you search for and implement a resolution?
A) Identify the problem
B) Test the theory to determine the cause
C) Establish a plan of action
D) Implement the solution

167. What is a crucial question to ask when trying to identify the problem?
A) How many people are affected?
B) What is the root cause?
C) What is the consequence of the problem?
D) How should we document the findings?

168. What should you do if a user describes symptoms such as error messages?
A) Implement the solution immediately
B) Navigate to the relevant log file and report on its contents
C) Ignore the symptoms
D) Escalate the issue

169. What is the final step in the CompTIA Troubleshooting Model?
A) Document findings/lessons learned
B) Verify full system functionality
C) Implement the solution
D) Establish a plan of action

170. Why is it important to be polite and patient when questioning users?
A) To gather accurate information
B) To escalate the issue
C) To implement the solution
D) To establish a new theory

171. What should you do if the user's problem has been intermittent for a few weeks but suddenly gets worse?

A) Focus your troubleshooting on recent changes

B) Ignore the problem

C) Implement the solution immediately

D) Document findings

172. Why is it helpful to observe the issue as it occurs?
A) To escalate the issue
B) To understand the problem better
C) To document findings
D) To implement preventive measures

173. What should you do if you do not recognize the problem after gathering information?
A) Ignore the problem
B) Use a product Knowledge Base or web search tool
C) Implement the solution immediately
D) Escalate the issue

174. When should you escalate an issue?
A) When the theory is confirmed
B) When the theory is not confirmed
C) Before identifying the problem
D) After implementing the solution

175. Why is it important to address questions to the user's level of expertise?
A) To blame the user
B) To gather accurate information
C) To escalate the issue
D) To implement the solution

176. Which of the following describes the primary function of a hypervisor?

A) It monitors network traffic for suspicious activity.

B) It manages hardware resources for multiple virtual machines.

C) It provides an interface for software applications to communicate.

D) It encrypts data stored on a hard drive.

177. What command can you use to copy a file to a disk or send it by email?
A) Edit > Cut
B) Edit > Move to Folder
C) Edit > Copy to Folder
D) Send To

178. What is the importance of verifying full system functionality?
A) To gather information
B) To ensure the problem is fully resolved
C) To escalate the issue
D) To implement a new solution

179. When should you consider multiple approaches in troubleshooting?
A) When questioning users
B) When establishing a theory of probable cause
C) When documenting findings
D) When implementing the solution

180. What should you do if problems seem to be related?
A) Treat each issue as a separate case
B) Check for outstanding support or maintenance tickets
C) Ignore one of the problems
D) Implement the solution immediately

181. What is the first question to ask when a problem is reported?
A) What are the symptoms?
B) How many people are affected?
C) When did the problem first occur?
D) What might have changed?

182. Which of the following is a characteristic of agile software development methodologies?
A) Rigid phase-based approach

B) Extensive documentation

C) Incremental and iterative development

D) Long-term planning with fixed requirements

183. Why is it important to classify the problem's nature and scope?
 A) To escalate the issue
 B) To gather accurate information
 C) To determine the severity
 D) To implement the solution

184. What should you do if you find that a machine has not been receiving maintenance updates?
 A) Treat it as a separate case
 B) Ignore the problem
 C) Escalate the issue
 D) Focus on the relation to the reported problem

185. Why should you use a remote desktop tool during troubleshooting?
 A) To escalate the issue
 B) To observe the system in operation
 C) To document findings
 D) To implement the solution

186. What should you do after gathering sufficient information about a problem?
 A) Implement the solution immediately
 B) Establish a theory of probable cause
 C) Escalate the issue
 D) Document findings

187. What should you consider when establishing a theory of probable cause?
 A) Only the obvious
 B) Multiple approaches
 C) Ignoring the symptoms

D) Implementing preventive measures

188. What is the benefit of asking the user to navigate to the relevant log file?
A) To escalate the issue
B) To gather detailed information
C) To implement the solution
D) To document findings

189. Which of the following actions best demonstrates ethical behavior in IT?
A) Using company resources for personal projects
B) Sharing confidential client information with colleagues
C) Reporting a security vulnerability to the responsible party
D) Ignoring minor security flaws to avoid disrupting operations

190. What should you do if the user cannot do any work due to a problem?
A) Focus on resolving the consequence
B) Establish a theory of probable cause
C) Gather more information
D) Duplicate the problem

191. What is a search engine?
A) A type of web browser
B) A tool to help locate web pages
C) A software for managing databases
D) A type of operating system

192. How do search engines usually compile their database of information?
A) Manually by human editors
B) Automatically by software agents called robots or spiders
C) Through user submissions
D) By purchasing data from other companies

193. When using a search engine, what do users enter to find information?

A) URLs

B) Keywords

C) Email addresses

D) Passwords

194. Which of the following is not a widely used search engine?

A) Google

B) Bing

C) DuckDuckGo

D) Internet Explorer

195. What is one way to access Google for different countries?

A) Using a VPN

B) Changing the domain extension (e.g., .co.uk, .com.au)

C) Modifying browser settings

D) Installing different software

196. What happens if you type text into the address bar that does not match an actual web address?

A) The browser will display an error message

B) The browser will convert the text into a search using the default search provider

C) The browser will close automatically

D) The browser will ask for user confirmation

197. How can you change the default search provider in a browser?

A) By installing a new browser

B) By using browser settings or preferences

C) By clearing browser cookies

D) By restarting the computer

198. What should you avoid using in search phrases to limit the number of matches?

A) Uncommon words

B) Specific dates

C) Common words such as "and" or "the"

D) Names of people

199. Which special syntax is used to specify a match to the exact phrase as you typed it?

A) +

B) -

C) OR

D) ""

200. What does the plus sign (+) in front of a word signify in a search query?

A) The word must be excluded

B) The word must be exactly found as typed

C) The word is optional

D) The word is a wildcard

201. How do you exclude a word from a search query?

A) Put the word in double quotation marks

B) Put a plus sign in front of the word

C) Put a minus sign in front of the word

D) Put the word in parentheses

202. What does the pipe (|) symbol mean in a search query?

A) Exclude either of the words

B) Include both words

C) Find either of the words

D) Match the exact phrase

203. In which context is the wildcard (*) used in search queries?

A) To exclude words

B) To represent unknown words between known ones

C) To specify exact phrases

D) To find either of the words

204. What can you use instead of syntax for advanced search criteria?
A) Browser extensions
B) Advanced Search page of the search engine
C) Incognito mode
D) Different search engines

205. What happens if you drag and drop an object without holding any keys to a local drive?
A) It copies the selection
B) It moves the selection
C) It creates a shortcut
D) It deletes the selection

206. What is the role of robots or spiders in a search engine?
A) To display search results
B) To compile a database of information about web pages
C) To update the web browser
D) To remove outdated web pages

207. How does a search engine return a list of relevant links?
A) By manually checking each web page
B) By comparing user-entered keywords against its database
C) By using user reviews
D) By contacting webmasters

208. What should you do to perform a search if you are unsure of the exact words?
A) Use wildcards (*)
B) Use only common words
C) Enter a single word
D) Include random characters

209. What is the purpose of the Advanced Search page on a search engine?
A) To install extensions
B) To specify criteria using a form

C) To update the search engine

D) To contact support

210. How can you specify that a word must be found in the title of a document in a search query?

A) Use double quotation marks

B) Use the word "intitle:"

C) Use a plus sign

D) Use a minus sign

211. What does "inurl:" specify in a search query?

A) The word must be in the URL of the document

B) The word must be in the title of the document

C) The word must be excluded from the search

D) The word must be optional

212. What is the result of using the minus sign (-) in a search query?

A) The word following the minus sign is a wildcard

B) The word following the minus sign is excluded

C) The word following the minus sign is optional

D) The word following the minus sign is treated as a phrase

213. What is the effect of using double quotation marks ("") around a phrase in a search query?

A) The words within the quotation marks are optional

B) The phrase is treated as a single word

C) The exact phrase must be matched

D) The phrase is excluded

214. Which of the following is an example of a low-level programming language?

A) Python

B) Java

C) Assembly language

D) JavaScript

215. What is the benefit of using more unusual words in a search phrase?
A) It increases the number of matches
B) It limits the number of matches
C) It makes the search more complex
D) It confuses the search engine

216. Which of the following is a correct example of using the wildcard (*) in a search query?
A) "Monty * Python"
B) "Monty + Python"
C) "Monty - Python"
D) "Monty | Python"

217. What happens if you do not use any special syntax in a search query?
A) The search engine will ignore the query
B) The search engine will perform a basic search
C) The search engine will ask for more details
D) The search engine will return no results

218. What is the purpose of changing the default search provider in a browser?
A) To access search results faster
B) To customize the search experience
C) To block unwanted ads
D) To enhance browser security

219. Which domain extension would you use to access Google in Australia?
A) google.com
B) google.co.uk
C) google.co.za
D) google.com.au

220. What special syntax would you use to ensure a word is included in search results exactly as typed?

A) ""
B) +
C) -
D) OR

221. If you want to exclude the word "Python" from your search results, which syntax would you use?
A) +Python
B) -Python
C) "Python"
D) Python*

222. What does the OR keyword do in a search query?
A) Excludes the word following it
B) Ensures the word following it is included
C) Finds either of the words specified
D) Matches the exact phrase

223. How can you search for documents that include the word "genius" and also any unknown words between "snake" and "python"?
A) "genius snake python"
B) genius +snake +python
C) genius * snake * python
D) genius snake * python

224. If you want to search for the exact phrase "Monty Python," what syntax would you use?
A) Monty Python
B) "Monty Python"
C) +Monty +Python
D) Monty|Python

225. Which of the following describes the primary purpose of a kernel in an operating system?

A) Provides an interface for user applications

B) Manages system memory and processes
C) Controls hardware devices directly
D) Manages file systems and storage

226. Which search engine result page feature allows users to specify criteria using a form?
A) Incognito mode
B) Advanced Search page
C) Browser settings
D) Default search provider

227. What is the function of the search engine's database?
A) To store user data
B) To compile information about web pages
C) To manage advertisements
D) To update search algorithms

228. How can you find documents containing the words "snake" or "python"?
A) snake + python
B) "snake python"
C) snake | python
D) snake * python

229. Which type of network topology involves every device connecting to a central hub, where all data passes through this hub before reaching its destination?

A) Mesh
B) Bus
C) Star
D) Ring

230. What is the impact of using more words in a search phrase?
A) It narrows the search results
B) It broadens the search results

C) It confuses the search engine

D) It excludes certain websites

231. How can users perform more complex searches using a search engine?

A) By using special syntax and search engine tools

B) By clearing their browser cache

C) By using a single keyword

D) By updating their browser

232. What keyword would you use to find documents containing either "genius" or "python"?

A) genius + python

B) genius - python

C) genius * python

D) genius | python

233. Which of the following best describes the role of middleware in an IT environment?

A) It provides an interface for user applications to interact with hardware.

B) It offers services to applications beyond those available from the operating system.

C) It directly manages system memory and CPU resources.

D) It encrypts data to ensure secure transmission.

234. How can you ensure that a word is found within a particular field, such as the document's URL?

A) Use the word in double quotation marks

B) Use the special syntax "inurl:"

C) Use a plus sign before the word

D) Use a minus sign before the word

235. What does the special syntax "+" signify in a search query?

A) The word must be excluded

B) The word must be optional

C) The word must be exactly found as typed

D) The word is a wildcard

236. What does collaboration software allow multiple users to do?
A) Play games together
B) Work together on the same file or project
C) Send instant messages
D) Create vector-based artwork

237. Which application allows users to compose and send messages, and also receive messages from others?
A) Remote Desktop Software
B) Email Software
C) Video Conferencing Software
D) Desktop Publishing Software

238. What feature does Personal Information Manager (PIM) software provide?
A) Storing and organizing information such as contacts and calendar events
B) Editing and formatting text documents
C) Creating bitmap artwork
D) Facilitating video conferences

239. What is an online workspace?
A) A place to create 3D animations
B) A file hosted on a network that users can access
C) Software for voice communications
D) A remote desktop server

240. What service does Microsoft SharePoint Server provide?
A) Instant messaging
B) Document storage and sharing
C) Graphic design
D) Voice over Internet Protocol (VoIP)

241. Which software is an example of cloud-based document storage and sharing?
A) Adobe Photoshop
B) Corel Painter
C) Google Drive
D) Microsoft Word

242. What does the "check out" feature in document editing do?
A) Allows multiple users to edit a document simultaneously
B) Locks the document for editing by other users
C) Creates a backup of the document
D) Deletes the document from the server

243. What is Remote Desktop software used for?
A) Connecting to a computer over a network
B) Creating digital drawings
C) Voice and video calling
D) Desktop publishing

244. What is the function of the remote desktop client application?
A) To edit bitmap artwork
B) To connect to a remote desktop server
C) To store and organize contact information
D) To facilitate video conferencing

245. What is a common use of remote desktops by IT support staff?
A) To create vector-based artwork
B) To login to a user's computer for support
C) To host online meetings
D) To prepare documents for professional printing

246. In a read-only mode, what can the remote user do?
A) Edit the host's desktop
B) View the host's desktop

C) Install the software on the host's computer

D) Delete files from the host's computer

247. What does Instant Messaging (IM) software allow users to do?
A) Send emails
B) Communicate in real time
C) Create 3D animations
D) Design web pages

248. What does Voice over Internet Protocol (VoIP) do?
A) Transmits voice communications as data packets
B) Facilitates screen sharing
C) Organizes calendar events
D) Edits photographic images

249. What are the requirements for implementing VoIP in a Peer-to-Peer configuration?
A) Graphic design software
B) Desktop publishing software
C) An internet connection, software, and a headset
D) A remote desktop server

250. What is latency in the context of IM software?
A) The delay in seconds that a data packet takes to travel over a network
B) The quality of the video in a conference call
C) The number of users connected to a network
D) The size of the files being transferred

251. What does video conferencing software allow users to configure?
A) Remote desktop connections
B) Virtual meeting rooms
C) Personal Information Managers
D) Graphic design projects

252. What does telepresence refer to in video conferencing?

A) The ability to edit documents online

B) The use of sophisticated video technologies for a real sense of presence

C) The creation of bitmap artwork

D) The transmission of voice over the Internet

253. What is the purpose of Desktop Publishing (DTP) software?

A) To assist with real-time communication

B) To format and layout documents for printing

C) To create 3D animations

D) To provide remote desktop connections

254. Which software is used for correcting and manipulating photographic images?

A) Adobe Illustrator

B) Adobe Photoshop

C) Corel Painter

D) Google Docs

255. What type of artwork can be resized without loss of quality?

A) Bitmap artwork

B) Vector artwork

C) 3D artwork

D) Animated artwork

256. What does the "master editor" do in document editing?

A) Approves and merges or rejects changes to a single published version

B) Creates a backup of the document

C) Locks the document for other users

D) Deletes the document from the server

257. In database management, what does ACID stand for?

A) Atomicity, Consistency, Isolation, Durability

B) Accessibility, Consistency, Isolation, Durability

C) Atomicity, Concurrency, Integrity, Durability

D) Accessibility, Concurrency, Integrity, Durability

258. What is the primary purpose of a remote desktop server?
A) To transmit voice communications
B) To host a desktop environment for remote access
C) To create vector-based line art
D) To format documents for printing

259. Which of the following is an example of a man-in-the-middle attack?

A) An attacker sends a phishing email to steal login credentials.
B) An attacker intercepts and alters communication between two parties without their knowledge.
C) An attacker floods a network with traffic to cause a denial of service.
D) An attacker installs malware to monitor keystrokes on a victim's computer.

260. What feature is crucial for real-time applications such as IM?
A) High latency
B) Sufficient bandwidth
C) Vector-based artwork
D) Desktop publishing tools

261. Which software allows the creation of bitmap artwork on a computer?
A) Adobe Photoshop
B) Corel Painter
C) Microsoft Word
D) Google Drive

262. What technology is used to achieve telepresence in video conferencing?
A) Vector-based line art
B) HD or 4K resolutions, large screens, and 3D
C) Remote desktop connections
D) Email and PIM software

263. What is a key feature of video conferencing software?

A) Creating digital drawings

B) Configuring virtual meeting rooms with voice, video, and IM

C) Formatting documents for printing

D) Storing and organizing contacts

264. Which software is used to create vector-based line art?

A) Adobe Photoshop

B) Corel Painter

C) Adobe Illustrator

D) Microsoft Word

265. What does Video Teleconferencing (VTC) software often include?

A) Screen sharing, presentation/whiteboard, file sharing, and polls/voting

B) Real-time text messaging

C) Bitmap artwork creation

D) Instant messaging and email integration

266. What type of artwork records the color value of each pixel in the image?

A) Vector artwork

B) Bitmap artwork

C) 3D artwork

D) Animated artwork

267. What is a requirement for good quality IM voice and video calling?

A) Low bandwidth

B) High latency

C) Sufficient bandwidth

D) Vector-based line art

268. What service is provided by Microsoft's OneDrive?

A) Creating bitmap artwork

B) Cloud storage and document sharing

C) Voice over Internet Protocol (VoIP)

D) Video conferencing

269. What is the purpose of digital darkroom products such as Adobe Photoshop?
 A) Correcting and manipulating photographic images
 B) Creating vector-based line art
 C) Facilitating remote desktop connections
 D) Communicating in real time

270. What is the role of teleconferencing in a video conferencing suite?
 A) A fallback option for voice or video calls if connection quality is poor
 B) A tool for creating 3D animations
 C) A feature for editing bitmap artwork
 D) A method for storing and organizing contacts

271. What is the typical use of remote desktop software for an ordinary user?
 A) To create vector-based line art
 B) To connect from a field laptop to a machine in the office
 C) To organize calendar events
 D) To format documents for printing

272. In the context of databases, which of the following normalization forms ensures that there are no transitive dependencies?
 A) First Normal Form (1NF)
 B) Second Normal Form (2NF)
 C) Third Normal Form (3NF)
 D) Boyce-Codd Normal Form (BCNF)

273. What does IM software require to function effectively?
 A) High latency
 B) Good quality network link
 C) Vector-based artwork software
 D) Desktop publishing tools

274. Which type of software is used for creating digital films or motion

picture effects?
A) Desktop Publishing Software
B) 3D and Animation Packages
C) Personal Information Manager (PIM)
D) Remote Desktop Software

275. What is a common feature of business software productivity suites?
A) Real-time voice and video communication
B) Performing a wide range of general office functions and tasks
C) Creating bitmap artwork
D) Facilitating remote desktop connections

276. What does the client software in an online workspace provide?
A) Tools to view and edit documents
B) Voice over Internet Protocol (VoIP) services
C) Instant messaging and video calling
D) Correcting photographic images

277. What is an example of a digital drawing product?
A) Google Docs
B) Adobe Illustrator
C) Microsoft SharePoint
D) Skype

278. What does a workspace server in an online workspace contain?
A) Tools for creating vector-based line art
B) Accounts and permissions of users allowed to access documents
C) Features for organizing contacts and calendar events
D) HD or 4K resolutions for video conferencing

279. What is the primary benefit of using specialized business software?
A) Facilitating voice and video calls
B) Assisting with specific business processes or consumer demands
C) Creating bitmap artwork
D) Hosting remote desktop sessions

280. What software is often used in conjunction with graphic design applications for web design?
A) Desktop Publishing Software
B) Personal Information Manager (PIM)
C) Video Conferencing Software
D) Remote Desktop Software

281. Which type of database stores information in a structured way?
A) Semi-structured
B) Unstructured
C) Relational
D) NoSQL

282. What is a characteristic of unstructured data?
A) Rigid formatting
B) Defined data types
C) Easier to create
D) Uses SQL

283. Which of the following is an example of semi-structured data?
A) SQL tables
B) XML documents
C) CSV files
D) Images

284. What type of database grows by adding documents to it without defining tables and fields?
A) Relational database
B) Document database
C) Key/Value pair database
D) NoSQL database

285. Which language is commonly used to provide structure in document databases?

A) SQL
B) JSON
C) XML
D) HTML

286. What does a key/value pair database store?
A) Tables
B) Documents
C) Properties of objects
D) Images

287. Which of the following is not a feature of relational databases?
A) Uses SQL
B) Predefined schema
C) Handles unstructured data
D) Structured data storage

288. What does the "CREATE" command do in SQL?
A) Deletes a table
B) Adds a new database
C) Modifies table columns
D) Retrieves data

289. Which command is used to delete a database in SQL?
A) DROP DATABASE
B) DELETE DATABASE
C) REMOVE DATABASE
D) ERASE DATABASE

290. What does the "INSERT INTO" command do in SQL?
 A) Updates a record
 B) Deletes a record
 C) Adds a new row
 D) Modifies table columns

291. Which command allows you to retrieve data from a database?
A) UPDATE
B) DELETE
C) SELECT
D) INSERT

292. What is the purpose of the "ALTER TABLE" command in SQL?
A) Add a new table
B) Delete a table
C) Modify table columns
D) Retrieve data

293. Which command is used to change the value of one or more table columns?
A) SELECT
B) DELETE
C) UPDATE
D) INSERT

294. How can you delete records from a table in SQL?
A) DROP TABLE
B) REMOVE RECORD
C) DELETE FROM
D) ERASE RECORD

295. Which of the following commands adds a new index to a column in SQL?
A) CREATE TABLE
B) CREATE INDEX
C) ADD INDEX
D) INSERT INDEX

296. What is the purpose of metadata in semi-structured data?
A) Provides rigid formatting
B) Helps identify the data

C) Defines table columns

D) Stores the primary key

297. Which of the following is a Data Definition Language (DDL) command?

A) SELECT

B) INSERT INTO

C) CREATE

D) UPDATE

298. What does the "DROP INDEX" command do in SQL?

A) Deletes a table

B) Removes an index

C) Adds an index

D) Updates a record

299. Which type of database is designed to handle a mixture of structured, unstructured, and semi-structured data?

A) Relational database

B) NoSQL database

C) Key/Value pair database

D) Document database

300. What does the "GRANT" statement do in SQL?

A) Deletes a table

B) Modifies table columns

C) Adds a new database

D) Grants specific rights to a user

301. Which software development methodology focuses on continuous feedback and improvement through iterative cycles and emphasizes customer collaboration?

A) Waterfall

B) Agile

C) V-Model

D) Spiral

302. Which of the following is not a Data Manipulation Language (DML) command?
A) INSERT INTO
B) UPDATE
C) DELETE FROM
D) CREATE INDEX

303. Which command is used to retrieve specific fields from a table in SQL?
A) SELECT * FROM
B) SELECT field1, field2 FROM
C) SELECT field1 field2
D) SELECT ALL

304. What does the "DENY" statement do in SQL?
A) Grants permission to a user
B) Denies permission to a user
C) Deletes a table
D) Modifies table columns

305. Which statement grants use of the SELECT statement to the user "James"?
A) GRANT SELECT ON Customers TO James
B) ALLOW SELECT ON Customers TO James
C) PERMIT SELECT ON Customers TO James
D) ENABLE SELECT ON Customers TO James

306. What is the command to remove all records from a table without deleting the table itself?
A) DELETE FROM TableName
B) DROP TABLE TableName
C) ERASE TABLE TableName
D) REMOVE ALL FROM TableName

307. Which statement retrieves all records from the "Customers" table where the "Town" field is "Slough"?
A) SELECT * FROM Customers WHERE Town='Slough'
B) SELECT * FROM Customers WHERE Town='Slough' ORDER BY Name
C) SELECT Town FROM Customers WHERE Town='Slough'
D) SELECT * FROM Customers WHERE Town=Slough

308. What is the result of the following SQL statement: SELECT * FROM Customers WHERE Town='Slough' ORDER BY Name?
A) Retrieves all records sorted by Town
B) Retrieves all records where Town is 'Slough' and sorts by Name
C) Retrieves all records where Name is 'Slough'
D) Retrieves all records sorted by Name

309. Which command would you use to add a new column to an existing table?
A) CREATE TABLE
B) ADD COLUMN
C) ALTER TABLE
D) INSERT INTO

310. Which of the following is an example of a key/value pair database format?
A) SQL
B) XML
C) JSON
D) HTML

311. What is the purpose of the "CREATE DATABASE" command?
A) Adds a new table
B) Adds a new database
C) Modifies table columns
D) Deletes a database

312. Which statement is true about NoSQL databases?
A) They only handle structured data
B) They use SQL as their primary query language
C) They can handle a variety of data types
D) They are a type of relational database

313. What does a Data Manipulation Language (DML) command do?
A) Defines database structure
B) Grants permissions
C) Manipulates data records
D) Creates indexes

314. Which command is used to change the owner of a database object?
A) ALTER AUTHORIZATION
B) CHANGE OWNER
C) UPDATE OWNER
D) MODIFY OWNER

315. What is an example of unstructured data?
A) SQL tables
B) XML documents
C) Word documents
D) JSON strings

316. Which type of database does not use a predefined schema?
A) Relational database
B) NoSQL database
C) SQL database
D) Structured database

317. What does the "UPDATE TableName" command do if no WHERE statement is specified?
A) Updates all records
B) Updates first record
C) Updates last record

D) Updates no records

318. What type of database is a document database?
A) Structured
B) Semi-structured
C) Unstructured
D) Relational

319. Which type of data provides no rigid formatting?
A) Structured
B) Semi-structured
C) Unstructured
D) Relational

320. Which command in SQL can be used to view data records?
A) SELECT
B) INSERT
C) DELETE
D) CREATE

321. What is the purpose of the "ALTER DATABASE" command?
A) Add a new table
B) Modify properties of the whole database
C) Delete a table
D) Retrieve data

322. In a key/value pair database, what does the key represent?
A) The data value
B) The unique identifier for the value
C) The table name
D) The database name

323. What does the "CREATE TABLE" command do in SQL?
A) Adds a new database
B) Adds a new table

C) Modifies table columns

D) Deletes a table

324. Which of the following is a widely used key/value format?

A) SQL

B) XML

C) JSON

D) HTML

325. What does denying permission using the "DENY" statement do?

A) Overrides GRANT permission

B) Grants permission to the owner

C) Deletes a table

D) Adds a new index

326. What is the primary function of the Central Processing Unit (CPU)?

A) Storing data

B) Displaying images

C) Running software programs

D) Managing network connections

327. What type of memory technology does system RAM use?

A) Flash memory

B) Magnetic disk

C) Random Access Memory (RAM)

D) Read-Only Memory (ROM)

328. Why is the speed of the memory subsystem important?

A) To ensure the computer can store more files

B) To match the speed of the CPU and prevent under-utilization

C) To enhance the display quality of images

D) To improve network connectivity

329. What happens to the programs and data when the computer is turned off?

A) They are permanently stored in system RAM

B) They are erased completely

C) They are stored on a Hard Disk Drive (HDD) or Solid State Drive (SSD)

D) They remain in the CPU

330. Which type of drive is faster for storing data?

A) HDD

B) SSD

C) ROM

D) RAM

331. What is a Graphics Processing Unit (GPU) primarily used for?

A) Running software programs

B) Managing network connections

C) Displaying high-resolution images and videos

D) Storing data

332. What type of connection is used in a wired network?

A) Wi-Fi

B) Bluetooth

C) Ethernet

D) Infrared

333. Where is the Network Interface Card (NIC) typically located in a workstation computer?

A) CPU

B) RAM

C) Motherboard

D) GPU

334. What does a motherboard determine in a computer?

A) The resolution of the display

B) The upgrade potential of the computer

C) The speed of the internet connection

D) The type of operating system installed

335. What is the primary function of the chipset on the motherboard?
A) Storing data
B) Providing built-in functions such as graphics, audio, and network adapters
C) Running software programs
D) Managing user inputs

336. Which Intel CPU brand is considered the flagship series for desktop and mobile?
A) Pentium
B) Celeron
C) Atom
D) Core

337. What does the AMD Ryzen/Threadripper brand represent?
A) Budget CPUs
B) High-end enthusiast segment
C) Server-class CPUs
D) Low-power portable devices

338. What type of microarchitecture is used in ARM CPUs?
A) CISC with RISC enhancements
B) Complex Instruction Set Computing (CISC)
C) Reduced Instruction Set Computing (RISC)
D) Enhanced CISC (eCISC)

339. What is the function of virtual memory in a computer?
A) To increase the physical size of RAM
B) To store permanent data
C) To supplement system RAM using part of the hard disk
D) To enhance the display quality of images

340. Which of the following is not a type of Intel CPU brand?
A) Xeon
B) Core

C) Ryzen

D) Celeron

341. What is the purpose of the Front Side Bus (FSB)?
A) To connect the CPU to the network
B) To connect the CPU to system memory
C) To connect the CPU to the GPU
D) To connect the CPU to the hard disk

342. Why might an add-on card be used on a computer?
A) To increase the size of the motherboard
B) To upgrade built-in functions such as graphics or network adapters
C) To store additional data
D) To enhance the CPU speed

343. What type of memory is used in Solid State Drives (SSD)?
A) Magnetic disk
B) Flash memory
C) Random Access Memory (RAM)
D) Read-Only Memory (ROM)

344. Which component is referred to as the "brains" of a computer?
A) RAM
B) GPU
C) CPU
D) Hard disk

345. Which of the following IP addresses is reserved for loopback testing?

A) 127.0.0.1
B) 192.168.0.1
C) 10.0.0.1
D) 255.255.255.255

346. What is the role of the bus in a motherboard?
A) To store data permanently

B) To connect different components

C) To display high-resolution images

D) To run software programs

347. Which Intel CPU brand is targeted toward low-power portable devices?

A) Core

B) Pentium

C) Atom

D) Xeon

348. What does the term "multi-core support" refer to in CPU technology?

A) A CPU with multiple processing units

B) A CPU that supports multiple GPUs

C) A CPU with additional RAM

D) A CPU that can connect to multiple networks

349. How does the GPU differ from the CPU in terms of functionality?

A) The GPU stores data while the CPU runs programs

B) The GPU processes graphics while the CPU runs general software programs

C) The GPU manages network connections while the CPU processes instructions

D) The GPU controls the motherboard while the CPU manages memory

350. What type of network connection does an Ethernet port provide?

A) Wireless

B) Wired

C) Bluetooth

D) Infrared

351. Which AMD CPU brand is aimed at the server/workstation market?

A) Ryzen

B) Epyc

C) Threadripper

D) Atom

352. What is the function of the chipset on a motherboard?
A) To run software programs
B) To provide built-in functions such as graphics, audio, and networking
C) To store data permanently
D) To connect to the internet

353. What is a common use of a wireless network in home environments?
A) To connect multiple GPUs
B) To provide Wi-Fi access
C) To enhance the CPU speed
D) To store data

354. What type of cable is used for Ethernet connections?
A) USB
B) HDMI
C) RJ-45
D) VGA

355. What would make upgrading a motherboard rarely cost-effective?
A) The high cost of new motherboards
B) The difficulty in finding compatible components
C) The limited performance improvement
D) The complexity of installation

356. Which Intel CPU brand is known for being a budget option?
A) Core
B) Pentium
C) Celeron
D) Xeon

357. What is the primary advantage of a multi-core CPU?
A) Increased storage capacity
B) Enhanced graphics processing

C) Better multitasking ability

D) Improved network connectivity

358. Why might a high-end workstation use an Xeon CPU?

A) For low power consumption

B) For high-end gaming

C) For n-way multiprocessing and ECC memory support

D) For budget-friendly computing

359. What does ECC memory stand for?

A) Error-Correcting Code memory

B) Enhanced Computing Capacity memory

C) Efficient Computing Core memory

D) Extended Cache Control memory

360. Which of the following cryptographic techniques is primarily used to ensure data integrity?

A) Symmetric encryption

B) Asymmetric encryption

C) Hashing

D) Digital certificates

361. What is the primary function of an Internet router in a home network?

A) To run software programs

B) To store data

C) To combine the functions of a modem, router, Ethernet switch, and Wi-Fi access point

D) To enhance the CPU speed

362. Which AMD CPU brand has replaced the older AMD FX chips?

A) Ryzen/Threadripper

B) Epyc

C) Athlon

D) Turion

363. What does the term "RISC" stand for?
A) Reduced Instruction Set Computing
B) Rapid Integrated System Computing
C) Random Instruction Set Computing
D) Reliable Integrated System Computing

364. What is a key characteristic of RISC microarchitectures?
A) Simple instructions are processed very quickly
B) Complex instructions are processed slowly
C) High power consumption
D) Incompatibility with most software

365. Why is the compatibility of components with the motherboard important?
A) To ensure physical fit and communication with the chipset
B) To increase the size of the motherboard
C) To store more programs
D) To enhance the display quality

366. What type of instructions does a CPU process?
A) Complex and slow instructions
B) Simple and fast instructions
C) Only graphical instructions
D) Only network instructions

367. What does the term "die" refer to in the context of a processor?
A) The outer casing of the CPU
B) The wafer of silicon doped with metal oxide containing transistors and pathways
C) The cooling mechanism of the CPU
D) The socket on the motherboard

368. What is the main characteristic of Xeon CPU that differentiates it from its Core i counterparts?
A) Lower power consumption

B) Support for n-way multiprocessing and ECC memory
C) Higher clock speed
D) Smaller physical size

369. What is the primary purpose of the chipset on a motherboard?
A) To store data permanently
B) To provide built-in functions and manage communication between components
C) To run high-end software programs
D) To enhance the display quality

370. Which of the following is not a function of a home internet router?
A) Acting as a modem
B) Providing an Ethernet switch
C) Running software programs
D) Providing a Wi-Fi access point

371. Which of the following is required for a PC to support dual monitors?
A) A single graphics adapter with a single port
B) A single graphics adapter with two display ports
C) Any graphics adapter
D) A single monitor

372. What does the Duplicate these displays option do in a dual monitor setup?
A) Extends the desktop over both devices
B) Displays the desktop only on one device
C) Displays the same image on both devices
D) Turns off one of the displays

373. Which type of network topology offers the highest redundancy and fault tolerance?

A) Star
B) Ring
C) Bus

D) Mesh

374. What key combination allows you to quickly select a multi-monitor mode in Windows 10?
A) ALT+P
B) CTRL+P
C) START+P
D) SHIFT+P

375. What option should you select if you want to use only one of the two connected monitors?
A) Duplicate these displays
B) Extend these displays
C) Show only on 1 or Show only on 2
D) Use both displays

376. What tool can you use to configure touchscreen settings in Windows?
A) Display settings
B) Pen and Touch applet
C) Sound settings
D) Keyboard settings

377. What is the purpose of calibrating a touchscreen?
A) To adjust the brightness
B) To set up or calibrate touch points on the screen
C) To change the screen resolution
D) To update the touch drivers

378. What does the Pen and Touch applet allow you to configure?
A) Screen resolution
B) Audio settings
C) Gesture settings
D) Network settings

379. Which port is used for audio input from devices such as tape decks or

CD players?
A) Microphone input (pink)
B) Audio out (lime)
C) Audio in (light blue)
D) HDMI

380. What is the color of the microphone input jack on a standard sound card?
A) Light blue
B) Pink
C) Lime
D) Black

381. What is the purpose of the lime-colored audio-out jack?
A) Audio input
B) Microphone input
C) Rear speakers
D) Feeding into amplified speakers or headphones

382. Which audio jack is used for connecting rear speakers in a surround sound system?
A) Audio out (lime)
B) Audio out (black)
C) Audio out (orange)
D) Microphone input (pink)

383. What does the orange audio-out jack signify?
A) Rear speakers
B) Center speakers
C) Subwoofer
D) Side speakers

384. What type of digital interface do higher-end sound cards include?
A) USB
B) HDMI

C) S/PDIF

D) VGA

385. Which connector types can S/PDIF use?

A) 3.5 mm jack

B) RCA or fiber optic

C) HDMI

D) VGA

386. What is the primary function of a sound card's DSP chip?

A) Process data from the computer to output a signal to speakers and process audio input

B) Enhance video playback quality

C) Improve network connectivity

D) Increase storage capacity

387. Which companies are noted for their professional-level sound cards?

A) Creative and Terratec

B) RealTek and Turtle Beach

C) E-MU, Yamaha, and Creative

D) Intel and AMD

388. What is the main difference between analog and digital multimedia ports?

A) Analog ports are faster

B) Digital ports require conversion to analog

C) Analog signals need to be converted to digital to be processed by the computer

D) Digital ports are only for audio

389. What is an example of a device that uses both a microphone and headphones?

A) Speaker

B) Headset

C) Amplifier

D) Sound card

390. Which of the following protocols operates at the Network layer of the OSI model and is used to route packets between different networks?
A) TCP
B) UDP
C) IP
D) HTTP

391. Which mode extends the desktop over both devices in a dual monitor setup?
A) Duplicate these displays
B) Extend these displays
C) Show only on 1
D) Show only on 2

392. In a 5.1 surround sound system, how many speakers are there in total?
A) Three
B) Four
C) Five
D) Six

393. Which speakers are added in a 7.1 surround sound system compared to a 5.1 system?
A) Center speakers
B) Side speakers
C) Rear speakers
D) Subwoofer

394. What does calibration involve in the Tablet PC Settings?
A) Adjusting screen brightness
B) Touching the crosshair at different points of the screen
C) Changing the screen resolution
D) Setting up audio inputs

395. What does the Pen and Touch applet's tap-and-hold gesture trigger?
A) Left-mouse click
B) Right-mouse click
C) Double click
D) Scroll

396. Which software development lifecycle model emphasizes risk analysis and iterative refinement through multiple cycles?
A) Waterfall
B) Agile
C) Spiral
D) V-Model

397. Which of the following types of malware is designed to provide unauthorized access to a system by bypassing normal authentication mechanisms?

A) Virus
B) Worm
C) Trojan horse
D) Rootkit

398. Which of the following practices is crucial for maintaining data confidentiality when disposing of old computer hardware?
A) Reformatting the hard drive
B) Deleting all files from the hard drive
C) Physically destroying the hard drive
D) Performing a quick format on the hard drive

399. Which of the following is a characteristic of a solid-state drive (SSD) compared to a traditional hard disk drive (HDD)?
A) Higher power consumption
B) Slower data access speeds
C) No moving parts
D) Larger storage capacity at lower cost

400. Which vendor is known for consumer-level sound cards?
A) E-MU
B) Yamaha
C) Creative
D) Intel

401. What does extending the desktop over both devices allow you to do?
A) Use more screen "real estate"
B) Duplicate the desktop
C) Show the desktop on one device only
D) Turn off one of the monitors

402. Which type of audio equipment can be connected via a USB port or Bluetooth?
A) Analog microphones
B) Analog speakers
C) Digital microphones, headsets, and speakers
D) RCA connectors

403. How do you adjust the physical position of monitors in an extended display setup?
A) By changing the screen resolution
B) By dragging the display icons in the display settings
C) By calibrating the touchscreen
D) By using the Pen and Touch applet

404. Which of the following is a key advantage of using fiber optic cables for data transmission?

A) Resistance to electromagnetic interference
D) Lower cost compared to copper cables
C) Higher susceptibility to signal attenuation
D) Ease of installation

405. Which type of software testing is performed without executing the

code and involves reviewing and analyzing the software's static components?
A) Unit testing
B) Integration testing
C) Static testing
D) Regression testing

406. How can you configure dual monitors in Windows 10?
A) Using the Sound settings
B) Using the Display tab in the System node in the Settings app
C) Using the Network settings
D) Using the Keyboard settings

407. Which design pattern provides a way to access the elements of an aggregate object sequentially without exposing its underlying representation?
A) Singleton
B) Factory
C) Observer
D) Iterator

408. In a distributed computing environment, what is the primary purpose of the CAP theorem?
A) To define the maximum number of nodes in a distributed system
B) To establish principles for data consistency, availability, and partition tolerance
C) To optimize the performance of database queries
D) To ensure secure communication between distributed nodes

409. What is the benefit of using digital multimedia ports over analog ports?
A) They are cheaper
B) They reduce signal degradation
C) They are easier to connect
D) They do not require any conversion

410. Which mode in dual monitors is useful for design, publishing, and programming work?
A) Duplicate these displays
B) Extend these displays
C) Show only on 1
D) Show only on 2

411. What type of signal do higher-end sound cards' S/PDIF jacks carry?
A) Analog
B) Digital
C) VGA
D) HDMI

412. Which of the following RAID levels offers both redundancy and improved performance by stripping data across multiple disks and providing parity?
A) RAID 0
B) RAID 1
C) RAID 5
D) RAID 10

413. Which type of surround sound system includes a subwoofer?
A) 2.1 system
B) 3.1 system
C) 5.1 system
D) Stereo system

414. What is the function of the Tablet PC Settings applet?
A) To configure network settings
B) To calibrate the touchscreen and set orientation options
C) To adjust screen brightness
D) To update touch drivers

415. What type of signal do RCA connectors used by S/PDIF carry?

A) Analog
B) Digital
C) VGA
D) HDMI

416. What is the main storage area for programs and data when the computer is running?
A) Hard Disk Drive (HDD)
B) System Memory
C) Solid State Drive (SSD)
D) External Hard Drive

417. What type of memory is system memory?
A) Flash Memory
B) Non-Volatile Memory
C) Volatile Memory
D) Permanent Memory

418. Which component is essential for a PC to run multiple applications simultaneously?
A) Hard Disk Drive
B) System RAM
C) External Hard Drive
D) Network Attached Storage

419. What happens when there is not enough system RAM?
A) The computer shuts down
B) The system uses disk space as virtual memory
C) The system crashes
D) The computer stops recognizing peripherals

420. What type of RAM is used in system memory?
A) Static RAM (SRAM)
B) Dynamic RAM (DRAM)
C) Flash RAM

D) Read-Only Memory (ROM)

421. How does DRAM store each data bit?
A) As a magnetic charge
B) As an electrical charge
C) As a light pulse
D) As a mechanical switch

422. What must happen periodically to DRAM to preserve information?
A) Reboot the system
B) Refresh each cell
C) Update firmware
D) Run diagnostics

423. What type of DRAM has been used since the mid-1990s?
A) EDO RAM
B) RDRAM
C) Synchronous DRAM (SDRAM)
D) FPM RAM

424. What is the form factor that SDRAM for laptops uses?
A) DIMM
B) SIMM
C) RIMM
D) SO-DIMM

425. How many bits of information can SDRAM deliver to the CPU in each clock cycle?
A) 32 bits
B) 64 bits
C) 128 bits
D) 256 bits

426. If the bus is running at 66 MHz, what is the bandwidth available to the memory controller?

A) 4224 megabits per second

B) 528 megabits per second

C) 264 megabits per second

D) 128 megabits per second

427. What feature does Double Data Rate SDRAM (DDR SDRAM) have?

A) Single data transfer per cycle

B) Triple data transfer per cycle

C) Double data transfer per cycle

D) Quad data transfer per cycle

428. What is the drawback of DDR technology updates?

A) Reduced bandwidth

B) Increased latency

C) Higher power consumption

D) Lower reliability

429. What form factor does DDR3 SDRAM use?

A) 240-pin DIMM

B) 168-pin DIMM

C) 200-pin SO-DIMM

D) 144-pin SO-DIMM

430. Can DDR3 modules be used in a DDR4 motherboard?

A) Yes

B) No

C) Only with an adapter

D) Only in certain slots

431. What type of storage retains data even when the power is turned off?

A) Volatile Memory

B) Non-Volatile Memory

C) System Memory

D) Virtual Memory

432. What is the most widely used type of mass storage device?
A) SSD
B) HDD
C) NAS
D) USB drive

433. How is data encoded on an HDD?
A) Electrically
B) Magnetically
C) Optically
D) Mechanically

434. What are the two formats for HDDs?
A) 2.5" and 3.5"
B) 1.8" and 2.5"
C) 3" and 5"
D) 4" and 6"

435. What does RPM stand for in the context of HDDs?
A) Revolutions per minute
B) Reads per minute
C) Random access memory
D) Random pattern memory

436. What is a typical RPM for budget and midrange HDDs?
A) 5400 and 7200 RPM
B) 7200 and 10000 RPM
C) 10000 and 15000 RPM
D) 15000 and 20000 RPM

437. What does a high-performance HDD access time usually fall below?
A) 1 ms
B) 4 ms
C) 9 ms
D) 15 ms

438. What interface do modern PCs and laptops use for internal hard disks?
A) EIDE/PATA
B) SCSI
C) SATA
D) USB

439. What does NAS stand for?
A) Network Attached Storage
B) Non-volatile Access Storage
C) Network Access System
D) Non-volatile Attached Storage

440. What type of memory do SSDs use?
A) DRAM
B) SRAM
C) Flash memory
D) Magnetic memory

441. What is a notable characteristic of flash memory?
A) Volatile
B) Non-volatile
C) Requires constant power
D) Slow

442. What key combination should you use to create a shortcut while dragging and dropping?
A) CTRL+SHIFT
B) CTRL+ALT
C) ALT+SHIFT
D) ALT+CTRL

443. What is the purpose of the SSD portion in a hybrid drive?
 A) To store the OS

B) To function as a large cache

C) To store user data

D) To increase capacity

444. What form factor do SSDs use for better performance when installed as PCIe adapter cards?

A) 2.5"

B) 3.5"

C) M.2

D) USB-C

445. Which standard bandwidth is the slowest?

A) USB 3.1

B) Thunderbolt 2

C) USB 2

D) USB 3

446. How many SATA ports do most motherboards have?

A) At least 2

B) At least 4

C) At least 6

D) At least 8

447. What type of memory is referred to as "volatile"?

A) HDD

B) SSD

C) RAM

D) Flash memory

448. What type of memory is referred to as "non-volatile"?

A) RAM

B) HDD

C) DRAM

D) SDRAM

449. Which company is not listed as a major hard drive vendor?
A) Seagate
B) Western Digital
C) Kingston
D) Toshiba

450. Which of the following attack types involves tricking an authorized user into disclosing sensitive information or performing an action that compromises security?
A) Phishing
B) Denial-of-Service (DoS)
C) Man-in-the-Middle (MitM)
D) SQL Injection

Answers

1. **Answer:** B) Desktop

Explanation: Desktop computers are housed in cases that can sit on or under a desk. The primary function of a desktop computer case is to enclose and protect the sensitive internal components of the computer.

2. **Answer:** B) Workstation

Explanation: The terms PC, desktop computer, and workstation are often used interchangeably. While these terms may overlap in everyday usage, they each have distinct meanings and contexts when considering their technical specifications and intended use cases.

3. **Answer:** B) Workstation

Explanation: A workstation is a particularly powerful type of desktop computer. Workstations are built with high-performance components, including powerful processors (such as Intel Xeon or AMD Ryzen Threadripper CPUs), large amounts of RAM (often starting from 32GB and going up to several hundred GBs), and fast storage solutions (such as SSDs or NVMe drives).

4. **Answer:** B) Peripheral devices

Explanation: Peripheral devices are connected to the motherboard via ports aligned to holes in the case. Peripheral devices are external devices that are connected to a computer system to extend its functionality. These devices include keyboards, mice, printers, external storage drives, and many other entities.

5. **Answer:** B) Mouse

Explanation: A mouse is an essential peripheral device for input. The primary function of a mouse is to provide a precise and intuitive way to control the cursor on a computer screen.

6. **Answer:** B) Data processing speed

Explanation: A higher specification CPU improves data processing speed. CPU speed is often measured in gigahertz (GHz), indicating how many cycles or instructions the CPU can execute per second. Higher clock speeds mean the CPU can process instructions more quickly.

7. **Answer:** B) CPU speed

Explanation: The speed of the CPU determines the basic speed of a computer. While the CPU speed is critical, it is important to note that overall system performance also depends on other components such as RAM, storage (SSD/HDD), and the GPU.

8. **Answer:** A) Solid State Drive (SSD)

Explanation: SSDs are replacing legacy hard drives due to their better performance. SSDs offer significantly faster read and write speeds compared to HDDs. This results in faster boot times for the operating system, quicker application launches, and faster file transfers.

9. **Answer:** B) Server components are more powerful and reliable

Explanation: Servers use more powerful and reliable components compared to desktops. Servers are designed to perform specific tasks that require high reliability, availability, and scalability. As a result, they typically utilize more powerful and reliable components compared to desktop computers.

10. **Answer:** B) High-quality components and redundancy

Explanation: Servers achieve reliability through high-quality components and redundancy. Servers use components that are built to higher standards of quality and reliability compared to those used in consumer-grade computers.

11. **Answer:** C) Laptop

Explanation: A laptop integrates display, system components, and input/output devices within a single case. This integration maximizes portability while providing functionality comparable to traditional desktop computers for everyday computing tasks.

12. **Answer:** A) 1 to 4 kg

Explanation: Laptops typically weigh between 1 and 4 kg. The materials used in a laptop's construction also impact its weight. Laptops made from lightweight materials such as aluminum, magnesium alloys, or carbon fiber are typically lighter than those made from heavier materials such as steel or thick plastic.

13. **Answer:** B) Flat-panel display

Explanation: Laptops use flat-panel display technologies. Laptops utilize flat-panel display technologies primarily due to their thin profile, energy efficiency, and improved visual quality compared to older CRT (cathode ray tube) displays.

14. **Answer:** B) Internal battery packs

Explanation: Portable computers use internal battery packs as a power source. Most modern portable computers use rechargeable Lithium-Ion (Li-ion) batteries.

15. **Answer:** B) Wireless radio technologies

Explanation: Portable computers primarily use wireless radio technologies for networking due to their inherent portability and convenience.

16. **Answer:** B) Notebooks

Explanation: Smaller laptops are often described as notebooks. Notebooks are generally designed to be compact and lightweight, making them highly portable.

17. **Answer:** D) macOS

Explanation: Apple Macintosh computers use macOS. macOS is the operating system developed by Apple Inc. specifically for its line of Macintosh computers.

18. **Answer:** A) Components are contained within the monitor case

Explanation: All-in-one PCs (AIO PCs) have components contained within the monitor case, integrating the computer's functionality into a single unit.

19. **Answer:** B) Extra copies of components

Explanation: Servers use extra copies of components for fault tolerance, which is crucial for maintaining high availability and reliability in enterprise environments where continuous operation is essential.

20. **Answer:** B) Rack-mountable case

Explanation: Servers often use rack-mountable cases due to several practical advantages they offer in data centers and server rooms. Rack-mountable cases allow servers to be densely packed into standard-sized server racks.

21. **Answer:** B) Web server

Explanation: A web server is an example of a software server. A web server is a specialized software application designed to handle HTTP (Hypertext Transfer Protocol) requests from clients, typically web browsers, and serve web pages, files, and other resources to them.

22. **Answer:** B) Hybrid laptops

Explanation: Hybrid laptops can be used as a tablet. Hybrid laptops, also known as 2-in-1 laptops or convertible laptops, combine the functionality of a traditional laptop with that of a tablet.

23. **Answer:** D) Microsoft

Explanation: Microsoft is not a dominant player in the global PC market. Microsoft, as a company, primarily develops and licenses software rather than manufacturing PCs themselves.

24. **Answer:** B) Ergonomics

Explanation: The quality of peripherals affects the ergonomics of a computer. Ergonomics refers to the design and arrangement of equipment and devices in a way that minimizes discomfort and maximizes efficiency and safety for the user.

25. **Answer:** B) Ultrabook

Explanation: Ultrabooks meet Intel's specifications for performance, size/weight, and battery life. Ultrabooks are a category of high-performance laptops that meet specific criteria set by Intel, aimed at providing a balance of performance, portability, and battery life.

26. **Answer:** B) Main storage drive type and speed

Explanation: The type and speed of the main storage drive impact system speed. Upgrading from an HDD to an SSD, especially one with high read/write speeds, can result in a noticeable improvement in system responsiveness and user experience across various tasks and applications.

27. **Answer:** C) Printer

Answers

Explanation: A printer is an optional peripheral device for a desktop PC because its functionality is not essential for the basic operation of the computer.

28. **Answer:** B) To allow audio playback

Explanation: A sound card, also known as an audio card or audio interface, allows audio playback on a desktop PC. It serves as the intermediary between the computer's digital data and the audio equipment, such as speakers or headphones.

29. **Answer:** B) CPU speed and system memory

Explanation: The performance of a desktop PC is mainly determined by CPU speed and system memory. The CPU and RAM work closely together to execute instructions and process data.

30. **Answer:** B) More expensive and reliable

Explanation: Servers are more expensive and reliable compared to desktops due to several key factors that distinguish them in terms of design, components, and intended use in business environments.

31. **Answer:** B) Easy to expand and upgrade

Explanation: Rack-mountable server cases are easy to expand and upgrade, which makes them highly suitable for data centers and server rooms where scalability and flexibility are essential.

32. **Answer:** B) Store more data when switched off

Explanation: A higher capacity main storage drive allows a computer to store more data when switched off. The primary function of a storage drive is to store data persistently, meaning the data remains intact even when the computer is powered off.

VERSAtile Reads

33. **Answer:** D) Apple

Explanation: Apple ships Macintosh computers. Apple manufactures its Macintosh computers in various facilities worldwide, including its manufacturing plants and contracted manufacturers (such as Foxconn and Pegatron).

34. **Answer:** B) Modifiable design with various components

Explanation: A major advantage of desktop PCs is their modifiable design. It refers to the ease with which users can upgrade and customize various components and peripherals.

35. **Answer:** B) Desktop PC

Explanation: A desktop PC is typically used as a network client. A network client refers to any device or computer system that accesses resources, services, or information provided by a server over a network.

36. **Answer:** B) Can be used as a tablet

Explanation: Hybrid laptops can be used as a tablet. Hybrid laptops feature a flexible design that allows the screen to be rotated, flipped, or detached from the keyboard base.

37. **Answer:** B) View

Explanation: The View tab contains options affecting how folders and files are displayed and allows resetting view settings. These options allow users to customize their viewing experience and manage how files and folders are organized and presented.

38. **Answer:** B) Graphics subsystem type and speed

Explanation: The type and speed of the graphics subsystem, which includes the Graphics Processing Unit (GPU) and associated components, are important factors.

39. **Answer:** B) Output

Explanation: A printer is used for output in a desktop PC, enabling users to obtain physical copies of documents, images, and other digital content stored on their computers.

40. **Answer:** B) Server

Explanation: Servers often use special cases designed to fit into steel rack shelving systems. Rack-mountable servers maximize space utilization in data centers by vertically stacking multiple servers in a compact and organized manner.

41. **Answer:** C) Ultrabook

Explanation: Ultrabooks meet specific performance and size/weight criteria. These criteria were introduced to define a new class of laptops that offer a balance of performance, portability, and battery life.

42. **Answer:** B) Run applications and process data more quickly

Explanation: System memory allows a computer to run more applications and process data more quickly. When you open an application or launch a program on your computer, it loads into system memory (RAM) from the storage drive.

43. **Answer:** B) Mobility and ease of connectivity

Explanation: Wireless radio technologies provide mobility and ease of connectivity. These technologies utilize electromagnetic waves to transmit data wirelessly between devices.

44. **Answer:** B) Touchpad

Explanation: Laptops integrate a touchpad, unlike typical desktops. Laptops are designed to be compact and portable, making external peripherals such as a mouse less practical for everyday use on the go.

45. **Answer:** C) Translates and executes high-level code line by line

Explanation: An interpreter translates and executes high-level programming code line by line. Unlike a compiler, which translates the entire code into machine language at once before execution, an interpreter processes the code one line at a time, which allows for immediate execution and is useful for debugging. This method, however, can be slower than compiled code because the translation happens during each execution.

46. **Answer:** B) Server

Explanation: Servers support many users simultaneously. Servers are specialized computers designed to handle and manage large volumes of data, requests, and tasks from multiple users or client devices simultaneously.

47. **Answer:** B) Larger, more powerful laptops

Explanation: Larger, more powerful laptops are often called "desktop replacements." The term "desktop replacement" refers to larger and more powerful laptops that are designed to offer performance and capabilities comparable to traditional desktop computers.

48. **Answer:** C) Hard drive

Explanation: Hard drives are often duplicated in server systems for fault tolerance. This redundancy strategy typically involves two main approaches: RAID (Redundant Array of Independent Disks) and disk mirroring.

49. **Answer:** B) Serve web pages to users

Explanation: A web server serves web pages to users. Its primary function is to handle requests from clients (typically web browsers) and respond by delivering the requested web pages or files.

50. **Answer:** A) Original Equipment Manufacturer

Explanation: OEM stands for Original Equipment Manufacturer. An Original Equipment Manufacturer (OEM) is a company that produces components or products that are purchased by another company and integrated into their final product.

51. **Answer:** B) Keyboard

Explanation: A keyboard is typically used for data input in a desktop PC. Its main function is to allow users to input text, commands, and other data into the computer.

52. **Answer:** A) Runs Chrome OS

Explanation: Chromebooks run Chrome OS. Chrome OS is specifically designed to work seamlessly with Google's Chrome web browser, integrating web-based applications and cloud computing to provide a lightweight, fast, and secure computing experience.

53. **Answer:** C) 5 to 9 kg

Explanation: Desktop replacement laptops typically weigh between 5 and 9 kg. Desktop replacement laptops are a category of laptops designed to provide performance and capabilities similar to desktop computers while maintaining the portability of a laptop form factor.

54. **Answer:** A) Acer

Explanation: Acer is a strong player in the laptop and hybrid markets, known for its diverse range of products catering to various segments of consumers and professionals.

55. **Answer:** B) Notebook

Explanation: Smaller, lighter laptops are often described as notebooks. Notebooks usually feature screen sizes ranging from 10 to 14 inches diagonally, although some may have slightly larger or smaller displays.

56. **Answer:** B) Serve database queries to users

Explanation: A database server serves database queries to users. A database server is a specialized computer or software system that is designed to store and manage databases, as well as serve database queries to users or applications.

57. **Answer:** C) Laptop

Explanation: Laptops typically have built-in batteries. These batteries provide the necessary power for the laptop to operate independently from a direct power source (such as a wall outlet) for a certain duration.

58. **Answer:** C) Fiber optic cable

Explanation: Fiber optic cables are used for high-speed data transmission over both short and long distances. They are known for their high bandwidth capabilities and immunity to electromagnetic interference (EMI), making them ideal for environments with high EMI or where high-speed data transfer is required. Fiber optic cables use light to transmit data, which allows for faster transmission speeds compared to electrical signals used in coaxial or twisted pair cables.

59. **Answer:** D) Apple

Explanation: Apple is not listed as a dominant player in the server market. Apple primarily focuses on designing and manufacturing consumer electronics and personal computing devices.

60. **Answer:** B) Software that manages the hardware components of a computer

Explanation: A device driver is a specialized software that allows an operating system to communicate with hardware components of a computer. Drivers translate the OS commands into instructions that the hardware can understand and act upon. Without the appropriate drivers, the OS would not be able to utilize the hardware components efficiently or at all.

61. **Answer:** B) To serve as an interface between the user, hardware, and applications

Explanation: The OS provides interfaces between the hardware, application programs, and the user. By providing essential interfaces, management tools, and security features, the OS ensures that computing systems are functional, reliable, and secure.

62. **Answer:** B) Command-line interface

Explanation: The earliest operating systems for PCs, such as DOS, used a command-line interface. A CLI requires users to type commands as text into a terminal or command prompt.

63. **Answer:** A) WIMP interface

Explanation: Windows is described as a WIMP interface: Window, Icon, Menu, Pointing device. The WIMP interface—Windows, Icons, Menus, Pointing device—defines the foundational elements of graphical user interfaces that enable intuitive navigation, efficient interaction, and visual representation of digital information and tasks in operating systems such as Windows.

64. **Answer:** B) Core functions of the OS

Explanation: The kernel provides the core functions of the OS. The kernel is the central part of the operating system that manages the system's resources and provides the essential services required for other software (applications and system utilities) to run.

65. **Answer:** C) A driver

Explanation: Each hardware component requires a driver to work with the OS. Device drivers are software programs that enable the OS to communicate with and control hardware devices connected to the computer.

66. **Answer:** B) 32-bit and 64-bit

Explanation: Most CPUs released in the last few years can work in either 32-bit or 64-bit mode. CPUs that support 64-bit architecture are often backward compatible with 32-bit operating systems and applications. This allows users to run older software designed for 32-bit systems on a 64-bit CPU.

67. **Answer:** C) Both 64-bit and 32-bit operating systems

Explanation: A computer with a 64-bit CPU can run both 64-bit and 32-bit operating systems. The ability to run both 32-bit and 64-bit applications on a 64-bit OS provides flexibility and ensures compatibility with a wide range of software, including legacy applications that may still be in use.

68. **Answer:** A) Programs that allow users to perform different tasks

Explanation: Application software consists of programs that allow users to perform different tasks. Unlike system software, which manages the computer's hardware and provides a platform for running applications, application software serves the end user directly.

69. **Answer:** C) Remain compatible with previous generations of software and hardware

Explanation: Changes to an OS must be made carefully to remain compatible with previous generations of software and hardware. Many users and organizations rely on specific software applications to perform their tasks. If an OS update introduces changes that break compatibility with existing software, it can disrupt workflows and productivity.

70. **Answer:** B) Directory (or folder) structure

Explanation: The OS uses a directory (or folder) structure to organize files on a storage device. The directory structure is hierarchical, meaning it is organized in a tree-like structure with levels of folders or directories.

71. **Answer:** B) Microsoft Windows

Explanation: Microsoft Windows is an example of a workstation OS designed primarily for personal computers and workstations used by individual users or small groups within organizations.

72. **Answer:** C) Mobile Device OS

Explanation: A mobile device OS is designed for handheld devices. Mobile OSs are optimized for touchscreen input, allowing users to interact with the device through taps, swipes, and gestures.

73. **Answer:** B) iOS

Explanation: The principal mobile operating system developed by Apple is iOS. iOS is known for its intuitive and user-friendly interface, featuring a touchscreen-based interaction model.

74. **Answer:** C) Software packages to run network services

Explanation: A server OS is likely to include software packages to run network services. Server OSs include built-in tools and software packages to manage network configurations, such as assigning IP addresses, setting up DNS (Domain Name System), DHCP (Dynamic Host Configuration Protocol), and managing network interfaces.

75. **Answer:** B) A system where the programming code is freely available

Explanation: Open source means that the programming code is freely available. Users of open-source software have access to its source code, which is the human-readable form of the program that developers write and modify.

76. **Answer:** C) UNIX

Explanation: UNIX is an example of an open-source OS. UNIX was originally developed by AT&T Bell Labs and later by various organizations and institutions. It started as a proprietary operating system.

77. **Answer:** C) Firmware

Explanation: In an embedded system, the OS acts as firmware. Embedded systems are specialized computing systems designed to perform specific tasks or functions within larger systems or devices.

78. **Answer:** C) Real-Time Operating System (RTOS)

Explanation: Highly stable and reliable embedded OS platforms are often Real-Time Operating Systems (RTOS). RTOS platforms are designed to guarantee a deterministic response time for critical tasks.

79. **Answer:** A) Basic Input/Output System

Explanation: BIOS stands for Basic Input/Output System. BIOS is responsible for initializing and testing hardware components during the computer's startup process (booting).

80. **Answer:** C) UEFI

Explanation: Newer motherboards may use UEFI firmware. UEFI offers a more modern and sophisticated graphical interface compared to the text-based interfaces of traditional BIOS.

81. **Answer:** C) Embedded OS

Explanation: An embedded OS typically cannot be uninstalled and replaced with a different OS. Embedded OSs are often customized and optimized for specific hardware configurations and functionalities of the embedded system.

82. **Answer:** B) Simplified application development

Explanation: A common OS environment simplifies application development. A common OS environment provides developers with standardized development tools, libraries, and APIs (Application Programming Interfaces).

83. **Answer:** B) Performance monitoring tools

Explanation: An OS might provide performance monitoring tools to monitor system health and performance. Performance monitoring tools typically track and display metrics related to CPU usage, memory utilization, disk I/O operations, and network bandwidth consumption.

84. **Answer:** C) Server OS

Explanation: A server OS is designed to run on servers in business networks. Server OSs are designed to efficiently manage hardware resources such as CPU processing power, memory (RAM), disk storage, and network connectivity.

85. **Answer:** C) Highly specific function devices

Explanation: An embedded OS is typically used in devices designed for a highly specific function. Embedded OSs are tailored to meet the specific requirements of the embedded device's intended application or industry.

86. **Answer:** C) The "size" of the instructions the CPU can process

Explanation: A fundamental difference between computer systems is the "size" of the instructions the CPU can process. The instruction set architecture defines the set of instructions that a CPU can execute.

87. **Answer:** B) Access control management

Explanation: Access control management involves regularly reviewing and updating user access rights and permissions to ensure that each user has the minimum level of access necessary to perform their job functions, a principle known as the least privilege. This practice helps to reduce the risk of unauthorized access and potential security breaches by limiting access rights to the minimum required for operational duties.

88. **Answer:** B) Quickly and cost-effectively

Explanation: Open-source software claims to make improvements available quickly and cost-effectively. Open-source projects often have a large and diverse community of developers and contributors worldwide.

89. **Answer:** C) To enable the hardware components to function

Explanation: Drivers enable the hardware components to function correctly with the OS. Drivers act as intermediary software layers that translate generic commands from the operating system into specific instructions understood by the hardware.

90. **Answer:** C) 64-bit CPU operation at boot

Explanation: UEFI provides support for 64-bit CPU operation at boot. UEFI firmware can initialize and transition the CPU into its 64-bit Long Mode during the boot process.

91. **Answer:** B) Time-sensitive tasks

Explanation: Many embedded systems perform acutely time-sensitive tasks. Embedded systems often operate in real-time environments where tasks must be completed within specific deadlines or time constraints.

92. **Answer:** C) Windows

Explanation: Windows is described as using a WIMP interface. WIMP stands for Windows, Icons, Menus, Pointer (or Pointing device). It describes a Graphical User Interface (GUI) paradigm that has become standard in modern operating systems, including Microsoft Windows.

93. **Answer:** C) Frequent reboots

Explanation: Real-Time Operating Systems (RTOS) do not tolerate frequent reboots. Real-Time Operating Systems (RTOS) are designed with a primary focus on deterministic behavior and predictable timing. Unlike general-purpose operating systems (such as Windows, macOS, or Linux), which may tolerate occasional reboots or system restarts, RTOSs are typically deployed in environments where continuous operation and minimal downtime are critical requirements.

94. **Answer:** B) Core functions of the OS

Explanation: The kernel provides the core functions of the OS. The kernel manages the system's resources, such as the CPU, memory, and I/O devices, ensuring that each application and process gets the necessary resources to function properly.

95. **Answer:** D) Apple macOS

Explanation: Apple macOS is an example of a commercial OS. A commercial operating system is developed by a company or organization for sale or licensing to end-users or businesses.

96. **Answer:** B) Focus on application functions

Explanation: The OS allows application software developers to concentrate on application functions. The OS abstracts the complexities of hardware management (such as CPU scheduling, memory management, and device drivers) from application developers.

97. **Answer:** C) Can be uninstalled and replaced

Explanation: A common feature of workstation OS is that they can be uninstalled and replaced. Workstation OSes, such as Windows, macOS, and various Linux distributions, are designed to allow users to install them on compatible hardware as needed.

98. **Answer:** B) Configure and monitor the computer

Explanation: One role of utility software included with an OS is to configure and monitor the computer. Utility software provides interfaces and tools for configuring system settings such as display resolution, network settings, power management options, and accessibility features.

99. **Answer:** C) Low-level interface for the OS to control components

Explanation: Firmware in a PC provides a low-level interface to allow the OS to control the PC components. Firmware is responsible for initializing essential hardware components during the boot-up process.

100. **Answer:** A) To organize files on a storage device

Explanation: The primary role of directory structure in an OS is to organize and manage files on a storage device such as a hard drive, SSD, or other types of storage media.

101. **Answer:** B) 64-bit editions

Explanation: Only 64-bit editions of Windows can run most 32-bit applications. 64-bit Windows can access more than 4GB of RAM, which is the maximum addressable memory for 32-bit systems. This allows for better performance and multitasking capabilities.

102. **Answer:** B) 64-bit hardware device drivers authorized by Microsoft

Explanation: 64-bit editions of Windows require 64-bit hardware device drivers authorized by Microsoft. 64-bit versions of Windows are designed to take advantage of the enhanced performance and capabilities of 64-bit processors and hardware.

103. **Answer:** B) No

Explanation: A 32-bit version of Windows cannot run 64-bit applications. 32-bit and 64-bit refer to the processing architecture of the CPU. A 32-bit Windows Operating System (OS) is designed to run on CPUs that are 32-bit. Similarly, a 64-bit Windows OS is designed for 64-bit CPUs.

104. **Answer:** A) Windows CE, Windows Phone 7, Windows Phone 8, and Windows 10 Mobile

Explanation: These are the mobile operating systems Microsoft has developed. These operating systems represented Microsoft's efforts to establish a presence in the mobile market. Still, they faced significant challenges competing against iOS and Android, ultimately leading to the discontinuation of Windows Phone and Windows 10 Mobile.

105. **Answer:** B) It is consistent across all types of devices

Explanation: Windows 10 Mobile has a consistent user interface and code base across all types of devices.

106. **Answer:** C) Apple

Explanation: The Apple Macintosh was developed by Apple. It was first introduced to the world on January 24, 1984, by Steve Jobs during a famous presentation.

107. **Answer:** B) It had a graphical user interface

Explanation: The Apple Macintosh was revolutionary for having a graphical user interface. Before the Macintosh, most personal computers used command-line interfaces where users had to type commands to perform tasks.

108. **Answer:** B) It is supplied only with Apple-built computers

Explanation: macOS is only supplied with Apple-built computers. macOS is designed to run exclusively on Apple's own hardware, such as MacBook laptops, iMac desktops, Mac Mini, and Mac Pro computers.

109. **Answer:** C) UNIX

Explanation: macOS was re-developed from the UNIX kernel. macOS is built on a Unix-like foundation, specifically derived from the Berkeley Software Distribution (BSD) variant of Unix.

110. **Answer:** B) Updates are released free-of-charge

Explanation: macOS updates are released to existing customers free of charge. Apple has a policy of offering macOS updates (both minor updates and major versions) at no cost to users who already own a compatible mac computer.

111. **Answer:** B) Its ease of navigation

Explanation: iOS is primarily known for its ease of navigation. iOS features a clean and intuitive user interface that is designed to be easy to understand and navigate, even for users who are not technically inclined.

112. **Answer:** B) Closed-source

Explanation: iOS is a closed-source operating system. iOS is proprietary software, meaning its source code is not publicly available for users or developers to view, modify, or distribute.

113. **Answer:** C) Entirely via touch

Explanation: The interface on an iPhone is controlled entirely via touch. The iPhone features a touchscreen display that responds to touch gestures such as tapping, swiping, pinching, and dragging.

114. **Answer:** B) To return the user to the Home Screen

Explanation: The Home key on an iPhone returns the user to the Home Screen. Newer iPhone models since the iPhone X no longer have a physical Home button.

115. **Answer:** C) UNIX

Explanation: Linux is based on the UNIX operating system. Linux is a Unix-like operating system, meaning it is inspired by and shares many similarities with the original Unix operating system developed in the 1970s at Bell Labs.

116. **Answer:** A) DEL

Explanation: Pressing DEL deletes the selected file. When you have a file or folder selected in Windows Explorer and press the "Delete" key on your keyboard, Windows prompts you with a confirmation dialog asking if you want to move the selected item to the Recycle Bin.

117. **Answer:** B) Minimal

Explanation: Chrome OS provides a minimal environment compared to Windows. Chrome OS is centered around the Google Chrome web browser. Most applications and tasks are designed to run within the browser environment, utilizing web apps and extensions available from the Chrome Web Store.

118. **Answer:** C) It is designed to use web applications

Explanation: Chrome OS was primarily developed to use web applications. Chrome OS encourages the use of web applications, which are accessed via the Chrome Web Store.

119. **Answer:** C) Google

Explanation: Chrome OS is developed by Google. Chrome OS was announced by Google in July 2009 and officially unveiled in November 2009.

120. **Answer:** B) Web servers

Explanation: Linux is very widely deployed on web servers. Linux distributions are generally open-source and free to use, which significantly reduces operating costs for web hosting providers and businesses.

121. **Answer:** A) Yes

Explanation: Chrome OS can run apps developed for Android. Most Android apps available on the Google Play Store can run on Chrome OS.

122. **Answer:** D) Windows XP Mobile

Explanation: Windows XP Mobile is not mentioned as a version of Windows for mobile devices. Windows Mobile was a family of operating systems developed by Microsoft for smartphones and Pocket PCs.

123. **Answer:** B) "Dot" version updates

Explanation: macOS gets periodic "dot" version updates. macOS updates are versioned using a numbering scheme that includes major releases (e.g., macOS Big Sur, macOS Catalina) and minor updates known as "dot" releases (e.g., macOS Big Sur 11.0, macOS Big Sur 11.1, macOS Big Sur 11.2, etc.).

124. **Answer:** B) Undo

Explanation: Shaking an iOS device activates undo. When you shake your iOS device (such as an iPhone or iPad), iOS interprets this motion as a request to undo the most recent action taken within an app.

125. **Answer:** B) Budget market

Explanation: Chrome OS hardware is designed for the budget market. Chromebooks typically use lower-cost components compared to traditional laptops running Windows or macOS.

126. **Answer:** B) The file will not open with the correct program

Explanation: Changing a file's extension can disassociate it from the correct program. When you double-click on a file, the operating system uses the file extension to determine which program to use to open it. If the file extension does not match the expected format of the file's contents, the operating system may not know how to interpret or open the file correctly.

127. **Answer:** B) CTRL+C

Explanation: CTRL+C is the keyboard shortcut for copying a file. After copying files using the appropriate keyboard shortcut, you typically use CTRL+V (or Command+V on macOS) to paste the copied files into the desired location.

128. **Answer:** B) It is derived from UNIX

Explanation: A key feature of Apple's OS X/macOS is that it is derived from UNIX. macOS is officially certified as UNIX by The Open Group. This certification ensures that macOS meets the standards and specifications required to be considered a UNIX operating system.

129. **Answer:** C) It helps to make Mac OS stable

Explanation: The main benefit of Mac OS being supplied only with Apple-built computers is that it helps to make Mac OS stable.

130. **Answer:** D) Microsoft

Explanation: Microsoft does not produce end-user applications for Linux. Microsoft historically focused on developing software primarily for its Windows operating system, with limited direct support for other operating systems such as Linux.

131. **Answer:** B) Web applications

Explanation: Chrome OS primarily uses web applications. Chrome OS users can access a wide range of applications through the Chrome Web Store.

132. **Answer:** A) As a server OS

Explanation: Linux is commonly used as a server OS in educational institutions. Linux distributions are open-source and free to use, which significantly reduces operating costs for educational institutions compared to proprietary server operating systems.

133. **Answer:** B) Free updates

Explanation: iOS updates are released free of charge. iOS updates are available to eligible devices through the Settings app under "General" and "Software Update."

134. **Answer:** B) Open-source

Explanation: Linux is considered to be an open-source operating system. Linux's source code is freely available to the public. This means that anyone can view, modify, and distribute the code according to the terms of its respective open-source license (most commonly the GNU General Public License or GPL).

135. **Answer:** B) macOS

Explanation: macOS is known for having a devoted following despite a smaller user base.

136. **Answer:** C) It is supplemented with additional code

Explanation: The macOS graphical interface is supplemented with additional code.

137. **Answer:** C) Touch

Explanation: The primary input method for iOS devices is touch. Users interact directly with the screen to control the device and navigate through apps and content.

138. **Answer:** B) Re-arrange icons

Explanation: By tapping and holding an icon on iOS, users can re-arrange icons. While in wiggle mode, you can drag app icons to different positions on the home screen or move them to different pages by dragging them to the edge of the screen.

139. **Answer:** C) Microsoft

Explanation: Microsoft produces Surface tablets, which are marketed as premium devices that integrate hardware and software designed to showcase Windows features and capabilities.

140. **Answer:** D) Android apps

Explanation: Besides web applications, Chrome OS can run Android apps. Google has integrated support for running Android applications on Chrome OS devices, expanding their functionality beyond just web-based applications.

141. **Answer:** B) UNIX

Explanation: The macOS kernel is developed from UNIX. Unix-based systems are known for their security and stability. macOS inherits these characteristics, providing a secure and reliable platform for users and developers.

142. **Answer:** B) Budget and affordable

Explanation: Chrome OS hardware is designed to be budget and affordable. Chromebooks typically utilize lower-cost hardware components compared to traditional laptops running Windows or macOS.

143. **Answer:** B) Web servers

Explanation: Linux is most widely deployed on web servers. Linux is renowned for its stability and reliability, making it suitable for running servers that need to operate continuously without frequent reboots or downtime.

144. **Answer:** B) Minimal and streamlined

Explanation: Chrome OS provides a minimal and streamlined environment, primarily focused on web-based tasks and applications.

145. **Answer:** D) Linux

Explanation: Unlike some other operating systems, such as Windows or macOS, Linux does not support a consistent user interface and code base across all device types.

146. **Answer:** B) Identify the problem

Explanation: The first step in the CompTIA Troubleshooting Model is to identify the problem. This may include asking questions to determine what changes occurred when the problem started and what errors or behaviors are observed.

147. **Answer:** C) Implement the solution

Explanation: Implementing the solution is not part of the step to identify the problem in the CompTIA Troubleshooting Model.

148. **Answer:** B) Resolving the consequences of the problem

Explanation: From a business point of view, resolving the consequences of the problem is often more important than solving the original cause.

149. **Answer:** B) Blaming the user for causing the problem

Explanation: Blaming the user should be avoided when questioning users. It can create a sense of distrust and reluctance to seek help in the future.

150. **Answer:** A) Establish a new theory or escalate

Explanation: If the theory is not confirmed, establish a new theory or escalate. If the initial theory is not confirmed through testing and analysis, revisit the information gathered and develop a new hypothesis about the probable cause of the problem.

151. **Answer:** C) Establish a plan of action

Explanation: Establishing a plan of action is not a technique used to identify the problem in the context of the CompTIA Troubleshooting Model.

152. **Answer:** B) To eliminate possible causes through testing

Explanation: The purpose of establishing a theory of probable cause is to eliminate possible causes one by one through testing.

153. **Answer:** A) Treat each issue as a separate case

Explanation: If you discover symptoms of more than one problem, treat each issue as a separate case. This approach is generally recommended in troubleshooting scenarios, especially when dealing with multiple symptoms or issues.

154. **Answer:** B) To identify potential causes of the problem

Explanation: Determining if anything has changed helps identify potential causes of the problem. It helps establish a timeline of events and potential triggers that may have led to the issue.

Answers

155. **Answer:** C) Verify full system functionality

Explanation: After implementing the solution, verify full system functionality. Verifying system functionality ensures that the problem identified has been effectively resolved.

156. **Answer:** B) Integer

Explanation: An integer is the most appropriate data type for storing a person's age in years because ages are whole numbers. Using an integer ensures that fractional values (which are inappropriate for age) are not stored, and it provides efficient storage and processing.

157. **Answer:** B) Configuration change

Explanation: Configuration change is a common cause of problems that occur after a change. Making changes to configuration settings, such as network configurations, application settings, or system preferences, can inadvertently introduce errors or misconfigurations.

158. **Answer:** C) Establish a plan of action

Explanation: After confirming the root cause, determine the next steps to resolve the problem by establishing a plan of action.

159. **Answer:** B) Identify the problem

Explanation: In any troubleshooting situation, the first action to take when encountering a troubleshooting situation is to identify the problem.

160. **Answer:** B) To gather information about the problem

Explanation: Questioning users helps gather information about the problem. Users often provide valuable information about the symptoms or behaviors they are experiencing.

161. **Answer:** B) F2

Explanation: Pressing F2 allows you to rename a file or folder. This keyboard shortcut is widely used because it provides a direct and efficient method to rename files or folders without needing to navigate through context menus or additional dialogs.

162. **Answer:** B) Focus on the user's local environment

Explanation: If the problem cannot be duplicated on a reference system, focus on the user's local environment. The user's local environment may have specific configurations, settings, or software versions that differ from the reference system.

163. **Answer:** B) SHIFT + ARROW keys

Explanation: Using SHIFT with the ARROW keys selects a block of files. This feature is useful when you need to quickly select multiple contiguous files or items in a list or grid view.

164. **Answer:** B) To identify similar problems

Explanation: Monitoring other support requests helps identify similar problems. By tracking and reviewing multiple support requests, you can identify recurring issues or patterns of problems that users are experiencing.

165. **Answer:** C) Question the user

Explanation: The first method to gather information about a problem is to question the user. Engaging with the user through questioning allows for immediate feedback and clarification of initial observations.

166. **Answer:** D) Implement the solution

Explanation: During the step to implement the solution, search for and implement a resolution. By searching for and implementing a resolution methodically during this step, troubleshooting efforts are focused on addressing the root cause of the problem and restoring normal system operation efficiently.

167. **Answer:** A) How many people are affected?

Explanation: Asking how many people are affected is crucial to determining the severity of the problem. It provides an initial indication of how widespread or localized the issue is within the organization or user base.

168. **Answer:** B) Navigate to the relevant log file and report on its contents

Explanation: If a user describes symptoms such as error messages, navigate to the relevant log file and report on its contents.

169. **Answer:** A) Document findings/lessons learned

Explanation: The final step in the CompTIA Troubleshooting Model is to document findings/lessons learned.

170. **Answer:** A) To gather accurate information

Explanation: Being polite and patient helps gather accurate information from the user. Politeness and patience help build a positive rapport with the user.

171. **Answer:** A) Focus your troubleshooting on recent changes

Explanation: If the problem has been intermittent but suddenly got worse, focus your troubleshooting on recent changes. Recent changes in software updates, configurations, or system settings can introduce new issues or exacerbate existing ones.

172. **Answer:** B) To understand the problem better

Explanation: Observing the issue as it occurs helps us understand the problem better. Observing the problem in real-time provides firsthand experience of how it manifests, including specific symptoms, error messages, or unexpected behaviors.

173. **Answer:** B) Use a product Knowledge Base or web search tool

Explanation: If you do not recognize the problem after gathering information, use a product Knowledge Base or web search tool.

174. **Answer:** B) When the theory is not confirmed

Explanation: Escalate an issue when the theory is not confirmed. If the issue is complex, involves specialized knowledge, or is beyond the expertise of the current support level, escalation allows the problem to be addressed by more experienced or specialized personnel.

175. **Answer:** B) To gather accurate information

Explanation: Addressing questions to the user's level of expertise helps gather accurate information. Tailoring questions to the user's level of expertise ensures that communication is clear, concise, and easily understood.

176. **Answer:** B) It manages hardware resources for multiple virtual machines.

Explanation: A hypervisor, also known as a virtual machine manager (VMM), is software that creates and manages virtual machines (VMs) by allocating hardware resources such as CPU, memory, and storage to each VM. The hypervisor allows multiple VMs to run concurrently on a single physical machine, each isolated from the others, enabling efficient use of hardware resources and improved flexibility in managing workloads.

177. **Answer:** D) Send To

Explanation: The Send To command can be used to copy a file to a disk or send it by email. Depending on your system configuration and installed applications, the "Send To" menu may offer additional options.

VERSAtile Reads

178. **Answer:** B) To ensure the problem is fully resolved

Explanation: Verifying full system functionality is a crucial step in the troubleshooting process to ensure that the problem is fully resolved.

179. **Answer:** B) When establishing a theory of probable cause

Explanation: It is essential to consider multiple approaches when establishing a theory of probable cause. This systematic approach not only strengthens troubleshooting skills but also promotes proactive problem management.

180. **Answer:** B) Check for outstanding support or maintenance tickets

Explanation: If problems seem to be related, check for outstanding support or maintenance tickets. Reviewing existing support tickets helps identify patterns or recurring issues that may be related to the current problem.

181. **Answer:** A) What are the symptoms?

Explanation: The first question to ask when a problem is reported is about the symptoms. Symptoms provide initial clues about the nature and scope of the problem.

182. **Answer:** C) Incremental and iterative development

Explanation: Agile software development methodologies emphasize incremental and iterative development, where the project is divided into small, manageable units called sprints or iterations. Each sprint delivers a potentially shippable product increment, allowing for continuous feedback and adaptation to changing requirements. This approach contrasts with traditional methodologies like Waterfall, which rely on rigid phase-based progress and extensive documentation.

183. **Answer:** C) To determine the severity

Explanation: Classifying the problem's nature and scope helps determine the severity.

184. **Answer:** D) Focus on the relation to the reported problem

Explanation: If a machine has not been receiving maintenance updates, focus on its relation to the reported problem.

185. **Answer:** B) To observe the system in operation

Explanation: Use a remote desktop tool to observe the system in operation. Remote desktop tools allow support technicians to view and interact with a user's desktop or server environment in real-time.

186. **Answer:** B) Establish a theory of probable cause

Explanation: After gathering sufficient information, establish a theory of probable cause. Thoroughly review all gathered information, including user reports, system logs, error messages, and any diagnostic data collected.

187. **Answer:** B) Multiple approaches

Explanation: Consider multiple approaches when establishing a theory of probable cause. Collect data from various sources such as users, system logs, error messages, and environmental factors.

188. **Answer:** B) To gather detailed information

Explanation: Asking the user to navigate to the relevant log file helps gather detailed information. By guiding the user to locate the specific log file related to the issue, you gain direct access to detailed information such as error messages, timestamps, and system events.

189. **Answer:** C) Reporting a security flaws to avoid disrupting operations

Explanation: Ethical behavior in IT includes taking responsibility for reporting security vulnerabilities to the appropriate parties to ensure they are addressed promptly. Ignoring or mishandling vulnerabilities can lead to significant risks and potential breaches. Reporting them helps protect the organization's data and maintains the integrity and security of its systems.

190.   **Answer:** A) Focus on resolving the consequence

Explanation: If the user cannot do any work, focus on resolving the consequence. Provide immediate assistance to mitigate the immediate consequence.

191.   **Answer:** B) A tool to help locate web pages

Explanation: A search engine helps users locate web pages on the internet. Search engines continuously crawl the web, gathering information from websites.

192.   **Answer:** B) Automatically by software agents called robots or spiders

Explanation: Search engines compile their database using software agents that crawl the web. As web crawlers visit a web page, they identify and follow links to other pages within the site and external sites. This process is known as crawling or spidering.

193.   **Answer:** B) Keywords

Explanation: Users enter keywords to find information on a search engine. Users type words, phrases, or questions related to what they are looking for into the search engine's search box. These are referred to as keywords or search queries.

194.   **Answer:** D) Internet Explorer

Explanation: Internet Explorer is a web browser, not a search engine. Internet Explorer is software used to access and view web pages on the Internet.

195. **Answer:** B) Changing the domain extension (e.g., .co.uk, .com.au)

Explanation: Different domain extensions are used to access Google in different countries. Google operates country-specific versions of its search engine for many countries around the world.

196. **Answer:** B) The browser will convert the text into a search using the default search provider

Explanation: If the text does not match a web address, it is converted into a search. This behavior is a feature implemented by most modern web browsers to enhance user experience and facilitate quick access to information.

197. **Answer:** B) By using browser settings or preferences

Explanation: You can change the default search provider in a browser's settings to customize your browsing experience.

198. **Answer:** C) Common words such as "and" or "the."

Explanation: Common words can increase the number of irrelevant matches. If a search query contains many common words, the search engine might focus less on meaningful keywords that could narrow down the results.

199. **Answer:** D) ""

Explanation: Double quotation marks specify an exact phrase match. When you enclose a phrase within double quotation marks in a search query, you instruct the search engine to find web pages where those words appear together and in the exact order specified.

200. **Answer:** B) The word must be exactly found as typed

Explanation: The plus sign ensures the word is exactly included as typed. In the context of search engines and search queries, the functionality of the plus sign (+) has evolved across different platforms. It may vary depending on the specific search engine's features and algorithms.

201. **Answer:** C) Put a minus sign in front of the word

Explanation: A minus sign excludes the word from the search. Placing a minus sign (-) directly before a word or phrase in a search query instructs the search engine to exclude results that contain that word or phrase.

202. **Answer:** C) Find either of the words

Explanation: The pipe symbol or the OR keyword is used to find either of the words. It serves as a Boolean operator that connects two or more terms in a search query.

203. **Answer:** B) To represent unknown words between known ones

Explanation: The wildcard (*) can represent unknown words. For example, searching for "comput" could match "computer," "computing," "compute," etc.

204. **Answer:** B) Advanced Search page of the search engine

Explanation: The Advanced Search page allows users to specify criteria without using syntax. The Advanced Search page typically offers a form-based interface with various fields and options that users can fill out or select.

205. **Answer:** B) It moves the selection

Explanation: The default action for drag and drop to a local drive is to move the selection. Understanding these default behaviors helps users manage their files efficiently and ensures that files are organized according to their intended actions during drag-and-drop operations.

206. **Answer:** B) To compile a database of information about web pages

Explanation: Robots or spiders crawl the web to build the search engine's database. Web crawlers start by visiting a list of known web pages or by following links from previously crawled pages.

207. **Answer:** B) By comparing user-entered keywords against its database

Explanation: The search engine checks keywords against its database to return relevant links. Search engines use web crawlers (or spiders) to systematically crawl and index web pages across the internet.

208. **Answer:** A) Use wildcards (*)

Explanation: Wildcards can help if you are unsure of the exact words. Wildcards allow you to specify placeholders for unknown characters within a word or phrase.

209. **Answer:** B) To specify criteria using a form

Explanation: The Advanced Search page allows users to enter specific criteria. Users can enter specific keywords, phrases, or combinations of terms to narrow down search results.

210. **Answer:** B) Use the word "intitle:"

Explanation: "intitle:" specifies that the word must appear in the title of the document. When you use the "intitle:" operator followed by a keyword or phrase, it instructs the search engine to return results where that specific word or phrase is included in the title of the document.

211. **Answer:** A) The word must be in the URL of the document

Explanation: "inurl:" ensures the word is in the URL of the document. When you use the "inurl:" operator followed by a keyword or phrase, it instructs the search engine to return results where that specific word or phrase is included somewhere within the URL of the webpage.

212. **Answer:** B) The word following the minus sign is excluded

Explanation: The minus sign excludes the word from the search results. For example, searching for "apple -fruit" would return results related to Apple Inc. but exclude results related to the fruit.

213. **Answer:** C) The exact phrase must be matched

Explanation: Double quotation marks ensure an exact phrase match. Placing a phrase within double quotation marks instructs the search engine to retrieve results that contain the exact sequence of words enclosed within the quotes.

214. **Answer:** C) Assembly language

Explanation: Assembly language is a low-level programming language that provides a symbolic representation of machine code instructions. It is closely related to the hardware architecture of the computer and requires a deep understanding of the processor and memory management. Low-level languages like Assembly offer fine-grained control over system resources, which is essential for performance-critical applications but is more complex and less portable compared to high-level languages like Python, Java, and JavaScript.

215. **Answer:** B) It limits the number of matches

Explanation: Using more unusual words narrows down the search results. Unusual or less common words are typically more specific in their meaning or context.

216. **Answer:** A) "Monty * Python"

Explanation: The wildcard represents unknown words between "Monty" and "Python." When you use a wildcard such as "*", it acts as a placeholder for any sequence of characters (including words) in a search query.

217. **Answer:** B) The search engine will perform a basic search

Explanation: Without special syntax, a basic search is performed. While advanced operators and syntax (such as quotation marks for exact phrases or wildcards for flexible matching) can enhance search precision and specificity, they are not required for conducting a basic search.

218. **Answer:** B) To customize the search experience

Explanation: Changing the default search provider customizes the search results. Most web browsers have a default search engine provider, such as Google, Bing, Yahoo, or others. This default provider determines where your search queries are sent and the results you receive.

219. **Answer:** D) google.com.au

Explanation: The domain extension for Google in Australia is google.com.au. This domain suffix indicates that the Google search engine is localized for users in Australia.

220. **Answer:** B) +

Explanation: The plus sign (+) ensures the word is exactly included as typed. For example, searching for "+apple" would ensure that results contained the word "apple."

221. **Answer:** B) –Python

Explanation: The minus sign (-) excludes the word "Python" from the search results. This feature is particularly useful when searching for topics with multiple meanings or when trying to filter out unrelated content.

222. **Answer:** C) Finds either of the words specified

Explanation: The OR keyword finds either of the words. The "OR" operator allows users to broaden their search queries by specifying multiple terms that may appear in search results.

223. **Answer:** D) genius snake * python

Explanation: The wildcard (*) represents unknown words between "snake" and "python." The asterisk (*) wildcard character can be used in search queries to find variations of a word or phrase where there may be unknown or variable words between specified terms.

224. **Answer:** B) "Monty Python"

Explanation: Double quotation marks ensure the exact phrase "Monty Python" is matched. Placing a phrase within double quotation marks instructs the search engine to retrieve results that contain the exact sequence of words enclosed within the quotes in the specified order.

225. **Answer:** B) Manages system memory and processes

Explanation: The kernel is the core component of an operating system responsible for managing system resources, including memory and processes. It ensures that applications can run simultaneously without interfering with each other by allocating CPU time and memory appropriately. It also handles system calls from user applications and manages hardware interactions indirectly through device drivers.

226. **Answer:** B) Advanced Search page

Explanation: The Advanced Search page allows specifying criteria using a form. The Advanced Search page presents users with a structured form that includes various fields and options to refine search queries.

227. **Answer:** B) To compile information about web pages

Explanation: The search engine's database stores information about web pages. The information collected by crawlers includes text content, HTML tags, links, images, and other elements present on the web page. This data is then processed and stored in the search engine's database.

228. **Answer:** C) snake | python

Explanation: The pipe (|) symbol finds documents containing either "snake" or "python." The pipe symbol (|) as an OR operator provides a powerful tool for expanding search criteria and combining multiple search terms to retrieve comprehensive and relevant information from databases, search engines, and programming contexts.

229. **Answer:** C) Star

Explanation: In a star topology, all devices are connected to a central hub or switch. The central hub acts as a conduit for data traffic; all data transmitted between devices on the network passes through this hub. This topology is easy to install and manage but can have a single point of failure at the hub, making it a critical component of the network's reliability.

230. **Answer:** A) It narrows the search results

Explanation: Using more words in a search phrase narrows down the results. Including more words in a search query often provides additional context and specificity, helping to refine the search results to be more relevant to the user's intent.

231. **Answer:** A) By using special syntax and search engine tools

Explanation: Special syntax and tools enable more complex searches, allowing users to refine and tailor their queries to retrieve specific and relevant information.

232. **Answer:** D) genius | python

VERSAtile Reads

Explanation: The pipe (|) symbol finds documents containing either "genius" or "python." When you use the pipe (|) symbol (in uppercase or its equivalent), it instructs the search engine to retrieve documents that contain either of the specified terms.

233. **Answer:** B) It offers services to applications beyond those available from the operating system.

Explanation: Middleware is software that provides common services and capabilities to applications outside of what's offered by the operating system. It acts as a bridge between applications and the underlying hardware or network. Middleware can include web servers, application servers, messaging systems, and database management systems, facilitating communication, input/output, and data management.

234. **Answer:** B) Use the special syntax "inurl:"

Explanation: "inurl:" ensures the word is found in the document's URL. It is a helpful tool for narrowing down search results based on the presence of keywords in the URL itself.

235. **Answer:** C) The word must be exactly found as typed

Explanation: The plus sign (+) is used to indicate that a word must be included in the search results exactly as typed.

236. **Answer:** B) Work together on the same file or project

Explanation: Collaboration software enables multiple users to work on the same file or project simultaneously. One of the key features of collaboration software is real-time editing capabilities.

237. **Answer:** B) Email Software

Explanation: Email software allows users to compose, send, and receive messages. Users can compose new messages directly within the email software interface.

238.   **Answer:** A) Storing and organizing information such as contacts and calendar events

Explanation: PIM software provides features for storing and organizing information such as contacts and calendar events.

239.   **Answer:** B) A file hosted on a network that users can access

Explanation: An online workspace hosts a file on a network, and users can sign in to access it. An online workspace typically refers to a virtual environment hosted on a network where users can collaborate, share files, and work together on projects.

240.   **Answer:** B) Document storage and sharing

Explanation: Microsoft SharePoint Server is a platform designed by Microsoft to facilitate document management, collaboration, and content sharing within organizations.

241.   **Answer:** C) Google Drive

Explanation: Google Drive is an example of a cloud-based document storage and sharing service. Google Drive allows users to store various types of files, including documents, spreadsheets, presentations, images, videos, and more, in the cloud.

242.   **Answer:** B) Locks the document for editing by other users

Explanation: The "check out" feature locks the document for editing by other users. This ensures that conflicting edits and version control issues are minimized.

243. **Answer:** A) Connecting to a computer over a network

Explanation: Remote Desktop software allows users to connect to and control a computer from another location over a network or the internet.

244. **Answer:** B) To connect to a remote desktop server

Explanation: In a remote desktop environment, the remote desktop client application connects to a remote desktop server to establish a remote connection and enable users to access and control the server's desktop interface from a different location.

245. **Answer:** B) To log in to a user's computer for support

Explanation: IT support staff commonly use remote desktop software to connect to a user's computer remotely and provide technical assistance or troubleshooting.

246. **Answer:** B) View the host's desktop

Explanation: In "read-only" mode, the remote user can view the host's desktop but cannot interact with it. This mode is useful for scenarios where the remote user needs to observe activities on the host's computer without making any changes or controlling the desktop interface.

247. **Answer:** B) Communicate in real time

Explanation: IM software allows users to communicate in real-time. IM software allows users to send and receive text messages instantly, facilitating rapid communication and collaboration.

248. **Answer:** A) Transmits voice communications as data packets

Explanation: Voice over Internet Protocol (VoIP) technology enables the transmission of voice communications as data packets over a network, typically the Internet or a private network.

249. **Answer:** C) An internet connection, software, and a headset

Explanation: VoIP in a Peer-to-Peer configuration requires an internet connection, software, and usually a headset. In a Peer-to-Peer (P2P) VoIP configuration, users communicate directly with each other over the Internet or another network without relying on a central server.

250. **Answer:** A) The delay in seconds that a data packet takes to travel over a network

Explanation: Latency refers to the delay in seconds that a data packet takes to travel over a network. It represents the time it takes for data to make a round trip from the source to the destination and back again.

251. **Answer:** B) Virtual meeting rooms

Explanation: Video conferencing software allows users to configure virtual meeting rooms. Users can create multiple virtual meeting rooms within the video conferencing platform.

252. **Answer:** B) The use of sophisticated video technologies for a real sense of presence

Explanation: Telepresence refers to the use of sophisticated video technologies to create a real sense of presence. The goal of telepresence systems is to simulate a realistic and immersive meeting experience where participants feel as if they are in the same room despite being geographically separated.

253. **Answer:** B) To format and layout documents for printing

Explanation: Desktop Publishing (DTP) software is used for formatting and layout of documents. DTP software allows users to design and arrange elements such as text, images, graphics, and multimedia components within a document.

254. **Answer:** B) Adobe Photoshop

Explanation: Adobe Photoshop is widely recognized and extensively used for correcting and manipulating photographic images.

255. **Answer:** B) Vector artwork

Explanation: Vector artwork can be resized without loss of quality. Unlike raster graphics (which are composed of pixels), vector graphics are based on mathematical formulas that define shapes, lines, curves, and colors.

256. **Answer:** A) Approves and merges or rejects changes to a single published version

Explanation: The master editor handles multiple revisions and approves and merges or rejects changes. This involves tracking changes made by editors or contributors, ensuring version control, and keeping a record of edits.

257. **Answer:** A) Atomicity, Consistency, Isolation, Durability

Explanation: ACID is a set of properties that ensure reliable processing of database transactions. Atomicity ensures that each transaction is all-or-nothing; Consistency ensures that a transaction brings the database from one valid state to another; Isolation ensures that transactions do not interfere with each other; Durability ensures that once a transaction is committed, it remains so, even in the case of a system failure.

258. **Answer:** B) To host a desktop environment for remote access

Explanation: A remote desktop server hosts a desktop environment that allows users to remotely access and control a computer or Virtual Machine (VM) over a network connection.

259. **Answer:** B) An attacker intercepts and alerts communication between two parties without their knowledge

Explanation: A man-in-the-middle (MitM) attack occurs when an attacker intercepts and potentially alters the communication between two parties without their knowledge. This can allow the attacker to eavesdrop on the conversation, steal sensitive information, or inject malicious data. MitM attacks can occur on both unencrypted and inadequately protected encrypted communications.

260. **Answer:** B) Sufficient bandwidth

Explanation: Real-time applications such as IM require sufficient bandwidth. Bandwidth refers to the maximum rate at which data can be transferred over a network connection.

261. **Answer:** B) Corel Painter

Explanation: Corel Painter is used to create bitmap artwork. Corel Painter is designed for artists, illustrators, and designers who want to create realistic and expressive digital paintings.

262. **Answer:** B) HD or 4K resolutions, large screens, and 3D

Explanation: Telepresence in video conferencing aims to create a highly immersive and lifelike experience by leveraging advanced technologies such as High-Definition (HD) or 4K resolutions, large screens, and sometimes even 3D capabilities.

263. **Answer:** B) Configuring virtual meeting rooms with voice, video, and IM

Explanation: Video conferencing software allows for configuring virtual meeting rooms with various options. Users can schedule meetings in advance, set dates and times, and send invitations to participants via email or calendar integration.

264. **Answer:** C) Adobe Illustrator

Explanation: Adobe Illustrator is used to create vector-based line art. Illustrator is designed for creating scalable vector artwork, which consists of mathematically defined geometric shapes (such as lines, curves, and polygons) rather than pixels.

265. **Answer:** A) Screen sharing, presentation/whiteboard, file sharing, and polls/voting

Explanation: VTC software often includes these features. These features collectively empower organizations and teams to conduct productive and interactive virtual meetings, training sessions, and collaborative activities.

266. **Answer:** B) Bitmap artwork

Explanation: Bitmap artwork, also known as raster graphics, records the color value of each pixel in the image. Each pixel contains specific color information, usually represented as a combination of Red, Green, and Blue (RGB) values.

267. **Answer:** C) Sufficient bandwidth

Explanation: Good quality IM voice and video calling require sufficient bandwidth. Sufficient bandwidth supports clear and uninterrupted audio transmission, allowing participants to hear each other with high fidelity.

268. **Answer:** B) Cloud storage and document sharing

Explanation: OneDrive provides cloud storage and document-sharing services. OneDrive provides users with online storage space where they can upload, store, and organize files such as documents, photos, videos, and more.

269. **Answer:** A) Correcting and manipulating photographic images

Explanation: Adobe Photoshop is used for correcting and manipulating photographic images. Photoshop provides powerful tools for basic to advanced image editing tasks, such as cropping, resizing, adjusting brightness and contrast, and applying filters to enhance or modify photos.

270. **Answer:** A) A fallback option for voice or video calls if connection quality is poor

Explanation: Teleconferencing, often referred to as audio conferencing or conference call, is used as a fallback option if IP voice or video call quality is poor.

271. **Answer:** B) To connect from a field laptop to a machine in the office

Explanation: Ordinary users use remote desktops to connect to office machines from remote locations. Many employees use remote desktops to access files, software applications, and other resources that are stored or installed on their office computers.

272. **Answer:** C) Third Normal Form (3NF)

Explanation: Third Normal Form (3NF) requires that a database is already in Second Normal Form (2NF) and that it contains no transitive dependencies. A transitive dependency exists when one non-key attribute depends on another non-key attribute. 3NF ensures that every non-key attribute is functionally dependent only on the primary key, thus reducing redundancy and improving data integrity.

273. **Answer:** B) Good quality network link

Explanation: Instant Messaging (IM) software, which facilitates real-time text-based communication between users, requires a good quality network link to function effectively.

274. **Answer:** B) 3D and Animation Packages

Explanation: 3D and Animation Packages are used to create digital films or motion picture effects. 3D packages allow artists to create three-dimensional models of characters, objects, environments, and scenes.

275. **Answer:** B) Performing a wide range of general office functions and tasks

Explanation: Business software productivity suites cover a wide range of general office functions and tasks. These suites typically include a combination of essential software tools that help businesses and individuals manage their day-to-day operations efficiently.

276. **Answer:** A) Tools to view and edit documents

Explanation: Client software in an online workspace provides tools to view and edit documents. They can view files such as text documents, spreadsheets, presentations, PDFs, and images directly within the application interface.

277. **Answer:** B) Adobe Illustrator

Explanation: Adobe Illustrator is a digital drawing product. Illustrator offers a wide range of drawing tools, including pen tools, shape tools, brush tools, and more.

278. **Answer:** B) Accounts and permissions of users allowed to access documents

Explanation: A workspace server contains the accounts and permissions of users allowed to access documents. Examples of workspace servers include Microsoft SharePoint Server, Google Workspace (formerly G Suite), Dropbox Business, and other enterprise-level collaboration platforms.

279. **Answer:** B) Assisting with specific business processes or consumer demands

Explanation: Specialized business software is designed to assist with specific business processes or consumer demands. Unlike general-purpose software, specialized software is designed to streamline and optimize specific business processes, improve efficiency, and address unique challenges faced by organizations.

280. **Answer:** A) Desktop Publishing Software

Explanation: Desktop Publishing Software is often used in conjunction with graphic design applications for web design.

281. **Answer:** C) Relational

Explanation: Relational databases are a type of Database Management System (DBMS) that store information in a structured way with defined data types and tables.

282. **Answer:** C) Easier to create

Explanation: Unstructured data, such as text files and images, provide no rigid formatting and are easier to create. Unstructured data refers to data that does not fit neatly into a traditional row-column database structure.

283. **Answer:** B) XML documents

Explanation: Semi-structured data includes XML documents that have associated metadata. Semi-structured data exhibits some structure, typically in the form of tags, keys, or markers that separate elements of the data.

284. **Answer:** B) Document database

Explanation: Document databases grow by adding documents without defining tables and fields. Document databases store data in documents, which are self-contained units of data containing key-value pairs or JSON-like structures.

285. **Answer:** C) XML

Explanation: XML (eXtensible Markup Language) is commonly used to provide structure in document databases. Document databases allow documents to have varying structures within the same collection, accommodating changes and updates without requiring schema migrations.

286. **Answer:** C) Properties of objects

Explanation: Key/value pair databases, also known as key-value stores, are a type of NoSQL (Not Only SQL) database that stores properties of objects without predetermining fields.

287. **Answer:** C) Handles unstructured data

Explanation: Relational databases do not handle unstructured data; they require structured data. Relational databases are designed to handle structured data, which means the data is organized and stored in predefined tables with rows and columns.

288. **Answer:** B) Adds a new database

Explanation: The "CREATE" command can be used to add new database objects such as databases, tables, indexes, views, and other schema elements.

289. **Answer:** A) DROP DATABASE

Explanation: The "DROP DATABASE" command deletes a database. It is used to delete an entire database along with all its objects, such as tables, views, indexes, and so on.

290. **Answer:** C) Adds a new row

Explanation: The "INSERT INTO" command adds a new row to a table. Users must have appropriate permissions to insert data into the specified table.

291. **Answer:** C) SELECT

Explanation: The "SELECT" command retrieves data from a database. It is one of the most fundamental and commonly used SQL commands for querying and retrieving specific information from tables.

292. **Answer:** C) Modify table columns

Explanation: The "ALTER TABLE" command allows modifications to table columns. This command allows you to add, modify, or drop columns, constraints, and indexes within a table.

293. **Answer:** C) UPDATE

Explanation: The "UPDATE" command changes the value of one or more table columns. You can update multiple columns simultaneously by specifying each column and its corresponding new value in the "SET" clause.

294. **Answer:** C) DELETE FROM

Explanation: The "DELETE FROM" command deletes records from a table. It allows you to remove one or more rows that meet a specified condition.

295. **Answer:** B) CREATE INDEX

Explanation: The "CREATE INDEX" command adds a new index to a column. Indexes are data structures that improve the speed of data retrieval operations on database tables by providing quick access paths to rows based on the indexed column(s).

296. **Answer:** B) Helps identify the data

Explanation: Metadata in semi-structured data helps identify the data. Semi-structured data refers to data that does not conform to a strict, predefined schema or structure, such as traditional relational databases.

297. **Answer:** C) CREATE

Explanation: The "CREATE" command is a Data Definition Language (DDL) command. DDL commands are used to define and manage the structure and schema of databases and database objects.

298. **Answer:** B) Removes an index

Explanation: The "DROP INDEX" command removes an index. Indexes in a database are data structures that improve the speed of data retrieval operations on tables by providing quick access paths to rows based on the indexed column(s).

299. **Answer:** B) NoSQL database

Explanation: NoSQL databases handle a mixture of structured, unstructured, and semi-structured data. NoSQL databases provide flexibility in data modeling and schema design, allowing developers to adapt to changing data requirements without rigid schema constraints.

300. **Answer:** D) Grants specific rights to a user

Explanation: The "GRANT" statement grants specific rights to a user. The "GRANT" statement is essential for controlling access to sensitive data and operations within a database system.

301. **Answer:** B) Agile

Explanation: Agile methodologies focus on iterative development, where requirements and solutions evolve through collaboration between self-organizing cross-functional teams. It emphasizes continuous feedback, customer collaboration, and flexibility to adapt to changing requirements. Agile methodologies like Scrum and Kanban promote frequent delivery of small, functional increments, allowing for constant improvement and alignment with customer needs.

302. **Answer:** D) CREATE INDEX

Explanation: "CREATE INDEX" is not a Data Manipulation Language (DML) command; it is a Data Definition Language (DDL) command.

303. **Answer:** B) SELECT field1, field2 FROM

Explanation: This command retrieves specific fields from a table. You can specify multiple fields separated by commas (field1, field2, ...) to retrieve more than two fields if needed.

304.   **Answer:** B) Denies permission to a user

Explanation: The "DENY" statement denies permission to a user. This statement is part of the access control mechanisms provided by Database Management Systems (DBMS) to enforce security policies.

305.   **Answer:** A) GRANT SELECT ON Customers TO James

Explanation: This statement grants the use of the SELECT statement to the user "James." This statement is used in SQL databases (such as MySQL, PostgreSQL, SQL Server, etc.) to control access and permissions to database objects such as tables, views, procedures, etc.

306.   **Answer:** A) DELETE FROM TableName

Explanation: The "DELETE FROM" command removes all records from a table without deleting the table. It removes rows (records) from the table based on the conditions specified or all rows if no conditions are provided.

307.   **Answer:** A) SELECT * FROM Customers WHERE Town='Slough'

Explanation: This retrieves all records where the "Town" field is "Slough." This SQL query is used to fetch data from a relational database (such as MySQL, PostgreSQL, SQL Server, etc.).

308.   **Answer:** B) Retrieves all records where Town is 'Slough' and sorts by Name

Explanation: This SQL statement retrieves records where the Town is 'Slough' and sorts them by Name. Town='Slough' specifies the condition. Here, it filters rows where the value in the "Town" column is equal to 'Slough'.

309. **Answer:** C) ALTER TABLE

Explanation: The "ALTER TABLE" command is used to add a new column to an existing table. The ALTER TABLE command can also be used for other modifications, such as renaming columns, dropping columns, or modifying column definitions (e.g., changing data types).

310. **Answer:** C) JSON

Explanation: JSON is an example of a widely used key/value pair database format. JSON is primarily used for transmitting data between a server and a web application, and it's often used in APIs (Application Programming Interfaces).

311. **Answer:** B) Adds a new database

Explanation: The "CREATE DATABASE" command adds a new database in a Database Management System (DBMS). Depending on the DBMS and user permissions, you may need administrative privileges to create databases.

312. **Answer:** C) They can handle a variety of data types

Explanation: NoSQL databases handle a variety of data types and are not limited to structured data. NoSQL (Not Only SQL) databases are a broad category of database management systems that are designed to handle various types of data models and structures.

313. **Answer:** C) Manipulates data records

Explanation: Data Manipulation Language (DML) commands manipulate data records. They allow users and applications to perform operations such as inserting, updating, deleting, and querying data records.

314. **Answer:** A) ALTER AUTHORIZATION

Explanation: The "ALTER AUTHORIZATION" command is used to change the owner of a database object. This command can be applied to various database objects such as tables, views, procedures, schemas, and databases themselves.

315. **Answer:** C) Word documents

Explanation: Word documents are an example of unstructured data. Unstructured data refers to data that does not have a predefined format or organization.

316. **Answer:** B) NoSQL database

Explanation: NoSQL databases do not use a predefined schema. Developers can store different types of data in the same database without needing to define a specific schema for each data type upfront.

317. **Answer:** A) Updates all records

Explanation: If no WHERE statement is specified, the "UPDATE" command updates all records. This means every row in the specified table will have its columns set to the new values specified in the SET clause.

318. **Answer:** B) Semi-structured

Explanation: Document databases are an example of semi-structured data. Semi-structured data refers to data that does not conform to the structure of traditional relational databases but has some organizational properties.

319. **Answer:** C) Unstructured

Explanation: Unstructured data provides no rigid formatting. Unstructured data lacks a rigid structure or schema that defines how the data should be organized or formatted. This makes it highly flexible but also challenging to manage using traditional database systems.

320. **Answer:** A) SELECT

Explanation: The "SELECT" command is used to view data records. It is a fundamental part of the Data Query Language (DQL) and allows users to specify which columns and rows of data they want to fetch.

321. **Answer:** B) Modify properties of the whole database

Explanation: The "ALTER DATABASE" command modifies properties of the whole database. It is part of the Data Definition Language (DDL) and allows administrators to change various aspects of a database, such as its name, collation, or state.

322. **Answer:** B) The unique identifier for the value

Explanation: In a key/value pair database, the key represents the unique identifier for the value. This type of database structure is straightforward and efficient for storing and retrieving data quickly based on its unique identifier.

323. **Answer:** B) Adds a new table

Explanation: The "CREATE TABLE" command is part of the Data Definition Language (DDL) and is used to add a new table. It allows database administrators to define the structure of a table by specifying its columns, data types, constraints, and other properties.

324. **Answer:** C) JSON

Explanation: JSON is a widely used key/value format. JSON is primarily used to represent structured data as key/value pairs. Each key is a string that maps to a value, which can be a string, number, object, array, Boolean, or null.

325. **Answer:** A) Overrides GRANT permission

Explanation: The "DENY" statement overrides GRANT permission. In SQL and database management systems, the DENY statement is used to explicitly deny specific permissions on database objects to a user or a group.

326. **Answer:** C) Running software programs

Explanation: The CPU processes instructions and directs other components to perform actions. The CPU retrieves instructions from the computer's memory (RAM).

327. **Answer:** C) Random Access Memory (RAM)

Explanation: System memory uses RAM technology. RAM consists of Integrated Circuits (ICs) that store data temporarily while the computer is powered on.

328. **Answer:** B) To match the speed of the CPU and prevent under-utilization

Explanation: The speed of the memory subsystem, particularly the RAM, is important to ensure the CPU is not under-utilized. If the RAM speed is slow, it can become a bottleneck, causing the CPU to wait longer for data and instructions to be fetched from memory.

329. **Answer:** C) They are stored on a Hard Disk Drive (HDD) or Solid State Drive (SSD)

Explanation: When the computer is turned off, data is stored on HDD or SSD. Both HDDs and SSDs are designed to retain data for extended periods without power.

330. **Answer:** B) SSD

Explanation: SSDs use flash memory and are much faster than HDDs. Integrating an SSD into a computer system can lead to faster boot times, quicker application launches, and smoother overall system responsiveness.

331. **Answer:** C) Displaying high-resolution images and videos

Explanation: The GPU is responsible for rendering images and videos. The GPU processes and renders visual data, including 2D and 3D graphics, animations, and videos.

332. **Answer:** C) Ethernet

Explanation: A wired network connection uses an Ethernet port. An Ethernet port, also known as an RJ45 port, is a standard interface found on network devices.

333. **Answer:** C) Motherboard

Explanation: The NIC is typically located on the motherboard. A NIC is a hardware component that enables a computer or device to connect to a network and communicate with other devices over that network.

334. **Answer:** B) The upgrade potential of the computer

Explanation: The motherboard determines what components can be upgraded. This includes the CPU (Central Processing Unit), RAM (Random Access Memory), GPU (Graphics Processing Unit), storage drives (HDDs and SSDs), and expansion cards.

335. **Answer:** B) Providing built-in functions such as graphics, audio, and network adapters

Explanation: The chipset supports various built-in functions and interfaces, facilitating communication between the CPU, memory, storage devices, expansion slots, and other peripherals connected to the motherboard.

336. **Answer:** D) Core

Explanation: Intel's Core series is the flagship CPU series. Intel's Core series CPUs are based on various microarchitectures, with recent generations including Skylake, Kaby Lake, Coffee Lake, Comet Lake, and, more recently, Tiger Lake and Alder Lake.

337. **Answer:** B) High-end enthusiast segment

Explanation: Ryzen/Threadripper represents AMD's high-end enthusiast CPUs. Ryzen and Threadripper are integral to AMD's strategy in providing competitive alternatives to Intel across various computing segments.

338. **Answer:** C) Reduced Instruction Set Computing (RISC)

Explanation: ARM CPUs use RISC microarchitecture. RISC architecture emphasizes simplicity and efficiency by using a smaller set of instructions that are executed with high speed and low latency.

339. **Answer:** C) To supplement system RAM using part of the hard disk

Explanation: Virtual memory uses part of the hard disk to supplement RAM. It provides a larger virtual address space than the physical RAM available in the system.

340. **Answer:** C) Ryzen

Explanation: Ryzen is an AMD brand, not Intel. Ryzen processors are designed and manufactured by AMD (Advanced Micro Devices), and they are known for their competitive performance, especially in the consumer and enthusiast markets.

341. **Answer:** B) To connect the CPU to system memory

Explanation: The Front Side Bus connects the CPU to system memory. The FSB acts as a communication pathway for data transfer between the CPU and system memory.

342. **Answer:** B) To upgrade built-in functions such as graphics or network adapters

Explanation: Add-on cards can upgrade built-in functions. Add-on cards, also known as expansion cards or peripheral cards, are hardware components that you can insert into expansion slots on the motherboard of a computer.

343. **Answer:** B) Flash memory

Explanation: SSDs use flash memory technology. Flash memory is non-volatile, meaning it retains data even when the power is turned off. This is crucial for storage devices such as SSDs, where data persistence is essential.

344. **Answer:** C) CPU

Explanation: The CPU is commonly referred to as the "brains" of the computer. The CPU is responsible for fetching instructions from memory, decoding them, and then executing them.

345. **Answer:** A) 127.0.0.1

Explanation: The IP address 127.0.0.1 is reserved for loopback testing in networking. It is used to test the network stack on the local machine without sending packets across the network. When a device sends data to 127.0.0.1, the data is looped back to the sender, allowing for testing and troubleshooting of the local network interface and software stack.

346. **Answer:** B) To connect different components

Explanation: The bus on the motherboard connects various components. The bus serves as a pathway or communication highway that connects the CPU (Central Processing Unit), memory (RAM), expansion slots, and other peripheral devices on the motherboard.

347. **Answer:** C) Atom

Explanation: Intel's Atom brand is for low-power portable devices, such as tablets, netbooks, and embedded systems. Intel introduced it to address the need for energy-efficient processors.

348. **Answer:** A) A CPU with multiple processing units

Explanation: Multi-core support means the CPU has multiple cores or processing units. Each core functions independently and can execute its instructions simultaneously with other cores.

349. **Answer:** B) The GPU processes graphics while the CPU runs general software programs

Explanation: The GPU handles graphics processing, while the CPU handles general instructions. In modern systems, both the CPU and GPU work together to provide a balanced computing experience, leveraging their respective strengths to ensure efficient performance across a wide range of applications and tasks.

350. **Answer:** B) Wired

Explanation: An Ethernet port is a hardware interface on a computer or other network device that provides a wired network connection.

351. **Answer:** B) Epyc

Explanation: Epyc is AMD's server-class CPU brand. AMD Epyc processors are designed for server and data center environments, where high performance, reliability, and scalability are crucial.

352. **Answer:** B) To provide built-in functions such as graphics, audio, and networking

Explanation: The chipset supports built-in functions on the motherboard. The chipset is responsible for coordinating communication between the CPU, memory, peripherals (such as USB ports and SATA ports), expansion slots (such as PCIe), and other components connected to the motherboard.

353. **Answer:** B) To provide Wi-Fi access

Explanation: Wireless networks in homes typically provide Wi-Fi access. Wi-Fi in homes is typically facilitated by wireless Access Points (APs) that connect to the home router or modem.

354. **Answer:** C) RJ-45

Explanation: Ethernet connections use cables with RJ-45 connectors. These connectors have eight pins and are designed to snap into the Ethernet port on a device, such as a computer, router, or switch.

355. **Answer:** A) The high cost of new motherboards

Explanation: Upgrading a motherboard is rarely cost-effective due to the high costs involved. New motherboards may require compatible CPUs, RAM, and other components. Upgrading these along with the motherboard can increase costs significantly.

356. **Answer:** C) Celeron

Explanation: Celeron is Intel's budget CPU brand. It is designed for entry-level computing tasks such as web browsing, basic office work, and light multimedia consumption.

357. **Answer:** C) Better multitasking ability

 Explanation: Multi-core CPUs improve multitasking by handling multiple tasks simultaneously. This capability significantly enhances overall system performance, especially in environments where users engage in tasks that require simultaneous processing.

358. **Answer:** C) For n-way multiprocessing and ECC memory support

Explanation: Xeon CPUs are used in high-end workstations for these features. The combination of n-way multiprocessing and ECC memory support ensures that these workstations can handle demanding tasks efficiently without compromising on data integrity or system stability.

359. **Answer:** A) Error-Correcting Code memory

Explanation: ECC memory stands for Error-Correcting Code memory. Error-Correcting Code (ECC) memory is a type of computer memory (RAM) that includes special circuitry to detect and correct memory errors automatically.

360. **Answer:** C) Hashing

Explanation: Hashing is a cryptographic technique used to ensure data integrity. It involves transforming data into a fixed-size hash value (or hash code) using a hash function. The hash value is unique to the original data, meaning any change in the data will result in a different hash value. This allows for the verification of data integrity by comparing hash values before and after transmission or storage, ensuring that the data has not been altered.

361. **Answer:** C) To combine the functions of a modem, router, Ethernet switch, and Wi-Fi access point

Explanation: Home internet routers often combine these functions. Having all functions in one device simplifies setup and reduces the number of devices needed.

362. **Answer:** A) Ryzen/Threadripper

Explanation: Ryzen/Threadripper has replaced older AMD FX chips. Ryzen and Threadripper processors have delivered substantial performance gains over the older FX series, particularly in single-threaded performance, multi-core efficiency, and overall computing power.

363. **Answer:** A) Reduced Instruction Set Computing

Explanation: RISC stands for Reduced Instruction Set Computing. It is a CPU design strategy that emphasizes a smaller set of simple and highly optimized instructions that can be executed very quickly.

364. **Answer:** A) Simple instructions are processed very quickly

Explanation: RISC microarchitectures use simple instructions processed quickly. This approach contrasts with Complex Instruction Set Computing (CISC), which includes a larger and more complex set of instructions.

365. **Answer:** A) To ensure physical fit and communication with the chipset

Explanation: Compatibility is important for physical fit and communication. Compatibility with the chipset and motherboard ensures that components not only physically fit but also communicate effectively, allowing the system to function optimally and reliably.

366. **Answer:** B) Simple and fast instructions

Explanation: The CPU processes simple and fast instructions. Modern CPUs often employ a combination of RISC and CISC principles, leveraging the strengths of each to achieve a balance between instruction set complexity and performance.

367. **Answer:** B) The wafer of silicon doped with metal oxide containing transistors and pathways

Explanation: The die refers to this part within the processor. The die is the physical component that houses the transistors, pathways, and other circuit elements necessary for the processor's functionality.

368. **Answer:** B) Support for n-way multiprocessing and ECC memory

Explanation: These features distinguish Xeon CPUs from Core i counterparts. Xeon CPUs are optimized for high-performance computing tasks in servers and workstations, offering robust multiprocessing capabilities and ECC memory support.

369. **Answer:** B) To provide built-in functions and manage communication between components

Explanation: The chipset provides built-in functions and manages component communication. The chipset plays a pivotal role in enabling seamless operation and interaction among various hardware components within a computer.

370. **Answer:** C) Running software programs

Explanation: Home Internet routers do not run software programs. These programs, often embedded in the device's firmware, control the router's operations, such as routing data between devices, managing Wi-Fi connections, providing security features such as firewalls, and allowing for configuration through a web interface.

371. **Answer:** B) A single graphics adapter with two display ports

Explanation: Dual monitors require either a graphics adapter with two display ports or two separate graphics adapters. In both scenarios, the setup enables you to extend your desktop across two monitors, providing more screen space and flexibility for multitasking, gaming, or other activities that benefit from dual-screen usage.

372. **Answer:** C) Displays the same image on both devices

Explanation: The "Duplicate these displays" option mirrors the same image on both monitors. This can be useful in situations where you want to share the same information or presentation across multiple screens, ensuring that both monitors display identical content.

373. **Answer:** D) Mesh

Explanation: In a mesh topology, each node is connected to multiple other nodes, often forming a fully interconnected network. This provides high redundancy and fault tolerance, as data can be rerouted through different paths if one connection fails. While this topology is more complex and expensive to implement, it ensures reliable communication and minimizes the risk of network downtime.

374. **Answer:** C) START+P

Explanation: Pressing START+P brings up the multi-monitor mode selection menu. The multi-monitor mode selection menu refers to the options available for configuring how multiple monitors connected to a computer display content.

375. **Answer:** C) Show only on 1 or Show only on 2

Explanation: This option allows you to display the desktop on only one of the connected monitors. By selecting "Show only on 1" or "Show only on 2", users can effectively control which monitor displays their desktop content, optimizing their workspace for specific tasks, presentations, or preferences.

376. **Answer:** B) Pen and Touch applet

Explanation: The Pen and Touch applet is used to configure touchscreen settings. This allows users to calibrate the touchscreen, adjust touch sensitivity, and configure other related settings.

377. **Answer:** B) To set up or calibrate touch points on the screen

Explanation: Calibration ensures the touch input is accurately mapped to the display. This process is important because it aligns the physical touch points on the screen with the digital coordinates that the operating system uses to interpret touch gestures.

378. **Answer:** C) Gesture settings

Explanation: The Pen and Touch applet allows you to configure gestures such as tap-and-hold. Users can access the Pen and Touch applet through the Control Panel or Settings menu, depending on the version of Windows.

379. **Answer:** C) Audio in (light blue)

Explanation: The light blue jack is used for audio input from devices such as tape decks or CD players. It accepts analog audio signals from external devices such as tape decks, CD players, or other audio equipment.

380. **Answer:** B) Pink

Explanation: The microphone input jack is typically pink. The use of pink for microphone input jacks is a standard color-coding convention across most consumer electronics, making it easy for users to identify and connect their microphones correctly.

381. **Answer:** D) Feeding into amplified speakers or headphones

Explanation: The lime-colored audio out jack is for outputting audio to amplified speakers or headphones. The lime jack typically supports stereo audio output. Stereo audio consists of two channels, left (L) and right (R), providing spatial sound separation for a more immersive audio experience.

382. **Answer:** B) Audio out (black)

Explanation: The black audio out jack is used for rear speakers in a surround sound system. Similar to the lime-colored audio out jack, the blackjack outputs line-level audio signals.

383. **Answer:** C) Subwoofer

Explanation: The orange audio out jack is for the subwoofer in a surround sound system. In a surround sound setup, the subwoofer is responsible for reproducing low-frequency sounds, such as deep bass tones and special effects.

384. **Answer:** C) S/PDIF

Explanation: Higher-end sound cards include a S/PDIF jack for digital audio signals. The S/PDIF jack allows for the transmission of digital audio signals between audio devices without the need for analog conversion.

385. **Answer:** B) RCA or fiber optic

Explanation: S/PDIF can use either RCA connectors or fiber optic cabling, providing flexibility in how digital audio signals are transmitted between devices.

386. **Answer:** A) Process data from the computer to output a signal to speakers and process audio input

Explanation: The DSP chip handles data processing for audio input and output. DSP chips excel at real-time processing of audio signals, ensuring minimal latency and high fidelity in both audio input and output scenarios.

387. **Answer:** C) E-MU, Yamaha, and Creative

Explanation: These companies are known for professional-level sound cards. They emphasize features such as high-resolution audio playback, low-latency recording, multiple input and output channels, and support for various audio formats and standards.

388. **Answer:** C) Analog signals need to be converted to digital to be processed by the computer

Explanation: Analog signals must be converted to digital for processing, which can degrade the signal. Analog signals, which are continuous and vary infinitely over time, need to be sampled and quantized into discrete digital values that can be processed and stored.

389. **Answer:** B) Headset

Explanation: A headset includes both a microphone and headphones. It is designed for audio communication, allowing the user to both listen to audio (such as music or voice) and speak into the microphone.

390. Answer: C) IP

Explanation: The Internet Protocol (IP) operates at the Network layer (Layer 3) of the OSI model. IP is responsible for routing packets between different networks by assigning unique IP addresses to each device and determining the best path for data to travel from the source to the destination. IP is a fundamental protocol for internetworking and provides the basis for the global Internet.

391. Answer: B) Extend these displays

Explanation: This mode extends the desktop across both monitors, increasing screen space. The extend mode enables users to use multiple monitors as one large desktop space.

392. Answer: D) Six

Explanation: A 5.1 system has six speakers: three front, two rear, and one subwoofer. A 5.1 audio system, also known as a 5.1 surround sound system, is a setup commonly used for home theater and multimedia experiences.

393. Answer: B) Side speakers

Explanation: A 7.1 system adds two side speakers to the 5.1 configuration. Audio content is divided into seven discrete channels (7 speakers + 1 subwoofer), ensuring a more detailed and immersive audio environment.

394. Answer: B) Touching the crosshair at different points of the screen

Explanation: Calibration involves touching points on the screen to set up touch accuracy. The device records the physical coordinates of where the user touches and compares them with the expected digital coordinates.

395. Answer: B) Right-mouse click

Explanation: The tap-and-hold gesture typically triggers a right-mouse click event in applications and operating systems that support it.

396. **Answer:** C) Spiral

Explanation: The Spiral model is a software development lifecycle model that emphasizes risk analysis and iterative refinement. It combines elements of both design and prototyping in stages, allowing for incremental improvements and risk assessment at each iteration. The model is divided into several cycles, each involving planning, risk analysis, engineering, and evaluation. This approach is particularly useful for large, complex, and high-risk projects.

397. **Answer:** D) Rootkit

Explanation: A rootkit is a type of malware designed to provide unauthorized access to a system by bypassing normal authentication mechanisms. Rootkits achieve this by altering system files and processes to hide their presence, allowing attackers to maintain persistent access to the system. They can operate at various levels, including the operating system and firmware, making them difficult to detect and remove.

398. **Answer:** C) Physically destroying the hard drive

Explanation: Physically destroying the hard drive is the most effective way to ensure data confidentiality when disposing of old computer hardware. While reformatting and deleting files can leave data recoverable through specialized tools, physical destruction (such as shredding or crushing) ensures that the data cannot be recovered. This method is recommended for sensitive or confidential information.

399. **Answer:** C) No moving parts

Explanation: A solid-state drive (SSD) has no moving parts, unlike a traditional hard disk drive (HDD), which relies on spinning disks and a moving read/write head. This lack of moving parts in SSDs results in faster data access speeds, greater durability, and lower power consumption. While SSDs tend to be more expensive per gigabyte and may have smaller storage capacities compared to HDDs, their performance benefits make them ideal for many applications.

400. **Answer:** C) Creative

Explanation: Creative is known for consumer-level sound cards. Creative's sound cards are known for their innovative features, high-quality audio output, and robust driver support, making them popular among gamers, audiophiles, and general users alike.

401. **Answer:** A) Use more screen "real estate"

Explanation: Extending the display allows for more workspace on the desktop. Extending the display is particularly useful for tasks that require multitasking or handling large amounts of information at once.

402. **Answer:** C) Digital microphones, headsets, and speakers

Explanation: Many digital audio devices can connect via USB or Bluetooth. Digital audio devices that support USB or Bluetooth connectivity are versatile and compatible with a wide range of devices and operating systems.

403. **Answer:** B) By dragging the display icons in the display settings

Explanation: You can adjust the physical position of monitors by dragging icons in the settings. This feature allows users to customize how the desktop spans across different monitors, ensuring optimal usability and viewing comfort based on their setup preferences.

404. **Answer:** A) Resistance to electromagnetic interference

Explanation: Fiber optic cables are highly resistant to electromagnetic interference (EMI) because they use light to transmit data rather than electrical signals. This resistance makes them ideal for environments with high levels of EMI, such as industrial settings or locations with heavy electrical equipment. Additionally, fiber optic cables can support higher bandwidths and longer distances without significant signal loss, although they are generally more expensive and challenging to install compared to copper cables.

405. Answer: C) Static testing

Explanation: Static testing involves reviewing and analyzing the software's static components (such as code, documentation, and design) without executing the code. This type of testing includes techniques like code reviews, walkthroughs, and inspections. Static testing helps identify potential defects early in the development process, improving software quality and reducing the cost of fixing issues later.

406. Answer: B) Using the Display tab in the System node in the Settings app

Explanation: Dual monitors can be configured using the Display settings in Windows. Dual monitors provide increased productivity by offering more screen real estate for multitasking, allowing you to spread out your work across multiple applications or view reference materials while working on a main task.

407. Answer: D) Iterator

Explanation: The Iterator design pattern provides a way to access the elements of an aggregate object sequentially without exposing its underlying representation. This pattern decouples the iteration logic from the aggregate object, allowing different traversal strategies to be implemented independently. The Iterator pattern is commonly used in collections and data structures to provide a standard way to iterate through their elements.

408. Answer: B) To establish principles for data consistency, availability, and partition tolerance

Explanation: The CAP theorem, also known as Brewer's theorem, states that in a distributed data store, it is impossible to simultaneously achieve all three of the following: Consistency (every read receives the most recent write), Availability (every request receives a response), and Partition Tolerance (the system continues to function despite network partitions). Systems must choose between consistency and availability when a partition occurs, hence guiding the design of distributed systems.

409. **Answer:** B) They reduce signal degradation

Explanation: Digital multimedia ports prevent signal degradation compared to analog ports. Digital multimedia ports, such as HDMI and DisplayPort, and digital audio interfaces, such as S/PDIF (Sony/Philips Digital Interface), offer superior signal quality, resistance to interference, and compatibility with modern audio and video standards.

410. **Answer:** B) Extend these displays

Explanation: Extending the display is useful for tasks that benefit from more screen space. Extended displays are also useful for presentations or collaborative work.

411. **Answer:** B) Digital

Explanation: S/PDIF jacks carry digital signals. S/PDIF carries audio data in a digital format using a protocol developed by Sony and Philips.

412. **Answer:** C) RAID 5

Explanation: RAID 5 provides both redundancy and improved performance by stripping data across multiple disks and using parity. In RAID 5, data and parity information are distributed across all disks in the array. This setup allows for data recovery in the event of a single disk failure while improving read performance due to striping. RAID 5 requires at least three disks and balances cost, performance, and redundancy effectively.

413. **Answer:** C) 5.1 system

Explanation: A 5.1 surround sound system includes a subwoofer. The subwoofer is responsible for reproducing low-frequency sounds, typically those below 120 Hz.

414. **Answer:** B) To calibrate the touchscreen and set orientation options

Explanation: The Tablet PC Settings applet is used for touchscreen calibration and orientation. The Tablet PC Settings applet in Windows is a utility designed primarily for configuring and optimizing the functionality of touchscreen devices.

415. **Answer:** B) Digital

Explanation: RCA connectors used by S/PDIF carry digital signals. These connectors are typically color-coded with white (left channel) and red (right channel) for stereo signals.

416. **Answer:** B) System Memory

Explanation: System memory, also known as RAM (Random Access Memory), is the main storage area for programs and data when the computer is running.

417. **Answer:** C) Volatile Memory

Explanation: System memory is a type of volatile memory called Random Access Memory (RAM). RAM is volatile, meaning it loses its stored information when the computer is powered off or restarted.

418. **Answer:** B) System RAM

Explanation: The size of RAM determines a computer's ability to work with multiple applications at the same time. Insufficient RAM can lead to performance bottlenecks because the operating system needs to compensate by using virtual memory (paging file) on the hard drive.

419. **Answer:** B) The system uses disk space as virtual memory

Explanation: If there is not enough system RAM, the memory space can be extended by using disk space (virtual memory). Virtual memory is slower than physical RAM, so excessive reliance on it can result in slower application response times.

420. **Answer:** B) Dynamic RAM (DRAM)

Explanation: System RAM is a type of RAM called Dynamic RAM (DRAM). DRAM requires periodic refreshing to maintain its data, hence the term "dynamic."

421. **Answer:** B) As an electrical charge

Explanation: DRAM stores each data bit as an electrical charge within a single-bit cell. The fundamental unit of storage in DRAM is a single-bit cell, which consists of a capacitor and a transistor. The transistor acts as a switch that controls access to the capacitor.

422. **Answer:** B) Refresh each cell

Explanation: Dynamic memory has to be refreshed periodically by accessing each cell at regular intervals. To ensure that the data stored in DRAM remains accurate and reliable, the memory controller periodically reads and rewrites the contents of each DRAM cell. This process is known as a refresh cycle.

423. **Answer:** C) Synchronous DRAM (SDRAM)

Explanation: Since the mid-1990s, variants of Synchronous DRAM (SDRAM) have been used for system memory. SDRAM aligns its internal operations with the system clock, ensuring data is transferred at precise intervals defined by the clock cycle.

424. **Answer:** D) SO-DIMM

Explanation: Laptops use a smaller form factor called Small Outline DIMM (SO-DIMM). Small Outline DIMM is a compact version of the standard DIMM (Dual Inline Memory Module) used in desktop computers.

425. **Answer:** B) 64 bits

Explanation: SDRAM has a 64-bit data bus, meaning that in each clock cycle, 64 bits of information can be delivered to the CPU.

426. **Answer:** A) 4224 megabits per second

Explanation: If the bus is running at 66 MHz, the bandwidth available to the memory controller is 66*64 or 4224 megabits per second.

427. **Answer:** C) Double data transfer per cycle

Explanation: Double Data Rate SDRAM (DDR SDRAM) features "double pumped" data transfers, meaning 64 bits at the start and end of each clock cycle.

428. **Answer:** B) Increased latency

Explanation: The drawback of DDR technology updates is increased latency. Latency refers to the time it takes for the memory module to respond to a data request from the CPU.

429. **Answer:** A) 240-pin DIMM

Explanation: DDR3 SDRAM (Double Data Rate 3 Synchronous Dynamic Random Access Memory) uses 240-pin DIMMs (Dual Inline Memory Modules).

430. **Answer:** B) No

Explanation: DDR3 modules cannot be used in a DDR4 motherboard due to different edge connector form factors.

431. Answer: B) Non-volatile memory

Explanation: Non-volatile storage retains its data when the power is turned off. The data remains intact until it is explicitly erased or overwritten by the user or the device's operation.

432. Answer: B) HDD

Explanation: Hard Disk Drives (HDD) are one of the most widely used types of mass storage devices. HDDs use magnetic storage to store and retrieve digital data.

433. Answer: B) Magnetically

Explanation: Data on an HDD is encoded magnetically. Each platter in an HDD is coated with a thin layer of magnetic material. This material can be magnetized in different directions to represent binary data—either a '0' or a '1'.

434. Answer: A) 2.5" and 3.5"

Explanation: HDDs come in 2.5" and 3.5" formats. 2.5-inch HDDs are smaller and more compact compared to their 3.5-inch counterparts.

435. Answer: A) Revolutions per minute

Explanation: RPM stands for revolutions per minute, a measure of how quickly the disks can spin. The faster the disks spin (measured in RPM), the quicker the read/write heads can access data stored on the platters.

436. Answer: A) 5400 and 7200 RPM

Explanation: Budget and midrange performance Hard Disk Drives (HDDs) typically have RPMs of 5400 and 7200. The choice between 5400 RPM and 7200 RPM HDDs depends on specific performance requirements and budget constraints.

437. **Answer:** B) 4 ms

Explanation: A high-performance HDD will have an access time below four milliseconds. Access time refers to the total time it takes for the HDD to locate and retrieve data from a specific location on the disk.

438. **Answer:** C) SATA

Explanation: Modern PCs and laptops use the SATA (Serial ATA) interface for internal hard disks. SATA is a computer bus interface that connects host bus adapters (such as motherboards and storage controllers) to mass storage devices such as Hard Disk Drives (HDDs) and Solid-State Drives (SSDs).

439. **Answer:** A) Network Attached Storage

Explanation: NAS stands for Network Attached Storage. NAS devices are designed to provide centralized storage and file-sharing functionalities to multiple users, computers, and devices within a network environment.

440. **Answer:** C) Flash memory

Explanation: Solid State Drives (SSD) use flash memory. Flash memory is organized into cells that store bits of data using electrically programmable transistors.

441. **Answer:** B) Non-Volatile

Explanation: Flash memory is non-volatile because it retains information without a power source. This is in contrast to volatile memory such as RAM, which loses its data when power is removed.

442. **Answer:** A) CTRL+SHIFT

Explanation: Holding CTRL+SHIFT while dragging and dropping creates a shortcut. Creating shortcuts in this manner allows you to access frequently used files or folders from multiple locations without duplicating the actual content.

443. **Answer:** B) To function as a large cache

Explanation: In a hybrid drive, the SSD portion functions as a large cache. A hybrid drive combines the traditional magnetic storage of a Hard Disk Drive (HDD) with a smaller Solid State Drive (SSD) component.

444. **Answer:** C) M.2

Explanation: Better performance is obtained from SSDs using the M.2 adapter interface, as the PCIe bus is much faster than SATA.

445. **Answer:** C) USB 2

Explanation: USB 2 has the slowest standard bandwidth at 480 Mbps. This speed represents the theoretical maximum data transfer rate under optimal conditions.

446. **Answer:** B) At least 4

Explanation: Most motherboards have at least four SATA ports. Having multiple SATA ports allows users to connect multiple storage devices to their motherboard, increasing the storage capacity and flexibility of the system.

447. **Answer:** C) RAM

Explanation: Volatile memory, such as RAM, requires a constant power source to retain information. When a computer is powered on, electricity flows through the RAM modules, keeping the memory cells energized. As long as the power is maintained, the RAM retains the data stored in it.

448. **Answer:** B) HDD

Explanation: Non-volatile memory, such as HDD, retains its data when the power is turned off. This characteristic makes it suitable for storing operating systems, applications, documents, and other files that need to be preserved even when the computer is not actively running.

449. **Answer:** C) Kingston

Explanation: Kingston is listed as a RAM vendor, not a major hard drive vendor. They have built a strong reputation for producing reliable and high-performance memory solutions for various computing platforms, including desktops, laptops, and servers.

450. **Answer:** A) Phishing

Explanation: Phishing is a type of social engineering attack that involves tricking an authorized user into disclosing sensitive information, such as usernames, passwords, or credit card numbers, or performing an action that compromises security. Attackers typically use email, text messages, or fake websites to impersonate legitimate entities and lure users into providing confidential information. Phishing is a common and effective attack vector because it exploits human psychology rather than technical vulnerabilities.

About Our Products

Other products from VERSAtile Reads are:

 Elevate Your Leadership: The 10 Must-Have Skills

 Elevate Your Leadership: 8 Effective Communication Skills

 Elevate Your Leadership: 10 Leadership Styles for Every Situation

 300+ PMP Practice Questions Aligned with PMBOK 7, Agile Methods, and Key Process Groups – 2024

 Exam-Cram Essentials Last-Minute Guide to Ace the PMP Exam - Your Express Guide featuring PMBOK® Guide

 Career Mastery Blueprint - Strategies for Success in Work and Business

 Memory Magic: Unraveling the Secret of Mind Mastery

 The Success Equation Psychological Foundations For Accomplishment

 Fairy Dust Chronicles – The Short and Sweet of Wonder

 B2B Breakthrough – Proven Strategies from Real-World Case Studies

CISSP Fast Track Master: CISSP Essentials for Exam Success

 CISA Fast Track Master: CISA Essentials for Exam Success

 CISM Fast Track Master: CISM Essentials for Exam Success

 CCSP Fast Track Master: CCSP Essentials for Exam Success

 CLF-C02: AWS Certified Cloud Practitioner: Fast Track to Exam Success

 ITIL 4 Foundation Essentials: Fast Track to Exam Success

 CCNP Security Essentials: Fast Track to Exam Success

 Certified SCRUM Master Exam Cram Essentials

 Six Sigma Green Belt Exam Cram: Essentials for Exam Success

 Microsoft 365 Fundamentals: Fast Track to Exam Success

 CKA Essentials: Fast Track to Exam Success

www.ingramcontent.com/pod-product-compliance
Lightning Source LLC
LaVergne TN
LVHW081342050326
832903LV00024B/1273